Dummies Guide to Starting a Business

The Simplified Beginners Guide to Launching a Successful Business

TABLE OF CONTENTS:

INTRODUCTION

Starting and growing a business is often seen as one of the most rewarding ways to earn a living, despite the challenges that come with it. To be a successful entrepreneur, you need more than just hard work and dedication. You also need a unique set of personality traits and business practices that are often found in successful people in this field. These traits are crucial in shaping the decisions that entrepreneurs make and influence the fundamental values and daily operations of their businesses.

Whether you're planning to start a new business or looking for ways to improve an existing one, this book will provide you with invaluable advice and guidance. By following the strategies outlined in this book, you can significantly increase your chances of starting a profitable business or revitalizing your current one.

Running a business is not always easy, but with the right mindset and a well-thought-out strategy, you can set yourself up for success. This involves carefully evaluating your needs, developing a robust business plan, and completing all the necessary legal paperwork before you start. Once you have a effective business strategy and the financial resources needed to achieve your goals, you'll be well on your way to launching a profitable and successful venture.

In the following sections of this book, we will explore the specific expectations that every business owner must meet to successfully create, manage, and grow their business or firm, both offline and online. Whether you're considering traditional brick-and-mortar options or venturing into the digital world, we'll provide you with the essential knowledge and tools to confidently and expertly navigate each realm.

Throughout this comprehensive guide, we'll cover important topics such as developing a winning mindset, conducting market research, creating compelling branding, implementing effective marketing strategies, managing finances, building exceptional teams, and scaling your business for long-term success.

By delving into these valuable insights, you'll gain a deep understanding of what it takes to succeed as an entrepreneur in today's dynamic business environment.

Remember, I stress this again and again: building and managing a successful business requires continuous learning, adaptation, and commitment.

This book aims to equip you with the knowledge and resources needed to overcome challenges, seize opportunities, and build a business that not only survives but thrives. So, prepare yourself for an enlightening journey that will enable you to realize your entrepreneurial dreams and take your business to unprecedented levels of success.

CHAPTER 1: THE ONE THING YOU NEED TO SUCCEED IN BUSINESS

If you have a unique skill that others lack, you might have the foundation to establish a business. Sometimes, all it takes is a readiness to offer a service or product that others can't or won't.

There are various motivations and methods to set up a business. Perhaps you're looking to diversify the revenue of an existing business. Maybe you're aiming to boost your earnings or desire to have more control over your life.

Many people assume that there's a single leap from their current situation to their desired goal. However, every aim is reached through a series of steps. If your first step is to follow the guidance of this book, your chances of success will significantly increase.

Your task is to figure out the necessary steps to practically achieve your goal, tailored to your startup. We might be tempted to skip a few steps to reach the exciting parts faster. But rest assured, if you follow and complete the steps, starting from the first one, your ascent will be more stable.

On the other hand, if you take the wrong initial step, you might miss your goal entirely.

When should you start a business?

A basic question many people ask is when is the right time to start a business? The best answer is the same as the answer to the question: When is the best time to plant a tree? Twenty years ago.

Some of us wait as if we're expecting a divine signal. Some of us wait for a significant event to act as a starting signal, like the sound of a starting gun. Others wait until they're in desperate situations with nothing left to lose, having already lost so much. It's better not to wait that long.

If something significant does happen, great, use it. However, often, something significant happens when you simply start, and your startup might just succeed.

The aim of this book is to motivate you to start sooner rather than later. If you fail, you'll learn from the failure.

What is your business?

Generally, businesses can be classified into service-based or product-based entities. These cover a wide range of industries, from agriculture to zoology, and everything in between. Your choice of business niche should be guided by your personal interests. If you don't enjoy your business, you're more likely to give up out of frustration or boredom when faced with challenges. Your passion for your industry will be the driving force that keeps you pushing forward, even in difficult times.

The Link Between Passion and Business

The excitement you feel for your business can be contagious, attracting potential clients, partners, suppliers, and coworkers. However, there's a catch; transforming your passion into a business can be a gamble. The business environment is always evolving, and your initial focus may not be what you end up concentrating on. For instance, you might begin with a love for cooking and professional culinary expertise, but realize that your business encompasses more than just cooking.

The Art of Customer Satisfaction in Business

The key to being a prosperous business owner lies in ensuring customer satisfaction. Using the cooking scenario, the quality of the food you prepare is the fundamental expectation of customers. To retain them and get them to recommend your business, you need to go the extra mile, build personal relationships with them, exceed their expectations, and establish proactive strategies to lure them back.

The Risk of Disruption in Outsourcing

Outsourcing tasks such as customer acquisition and management might seem appealing, but it also carries potential hazards. If you outsource a vital function and something goes wrong, your business could be adversely affected. Therefore, it's crucial to have a controlled process or system for essential tasks like customer acquisition and retention.

Business Fundamentals: Quality and Sales

No matter the nature of your business, the keys to success remain the same: efficient customer acquisition and management, quality assurance, and superior service or product. Even the most convincing salesperson cannot make up for a substandard product or service. This emphasizes the significance of having a knowledgeable sales team that understands not just the product, but also the client's needs.

Learning from Sales Failures

Sales can be a tough field, particularly if you or your team lack understanding about the services or the clients. A personal experience of losing a client due to a sales representative's misunderstanding demonstrates the importance of this knowledge. It also highlights the necessity for technical experts, like chefs in the culinary industry, to participate in customer management and expectation setting.

The Significance of Operational Processes

To grow your business, operational procedures for all areas, including production, quality, security, HR, and training, should be established. These procedures should be adaptable enough to accommodate various customer needs. After all, business success is about fulfilling customer demands, even if it strays from your original plans.

Adapting to Customer Needs

It's crucial for your business to adapt to the needs of your customers.

For example, if you're a pastry chef but your customers are asking for more diverse menu options, it would be wise to adjust your offerings accordingly. This adaptability is key to ensuring your business remains profitable and relevant.

The Experimental Nature of Business

Business operations can often feel like an ongoing experiment.

You may find that customers are drawn to your main services and recommend you to others based on their positive experiences. However, these new customers may have their own preconceived notions about what you offer. In these cases, it's important to clearly communicate your services, much like a chef would use a menu to inform customers about the dishes they serve.

If you're unsure about what type of business to start, there are resources available, such as the book "Discovered, 505 Odd Enterprises" by George Haylings, which can provide a wealth of ideas. The main point to remember is that your business should meet the demands of your customers.

Business Processes: The Backbone of Your Business

Efficient business processes are essential to running a successful business.

These processes, which encompass sales, production, delivery, and finance, ensure that your business operations function seamlessly. And at the core of these operations are your customers.

Understanding and Meeting Customer Needs

It's essential to understand what your customers want and to figure out how to provide it in a way that satisfies them.

Before anything else, your primary goal should be to secure your first paying customer. This could mean offering a simple product or service in exchange for payment. In many instances, this could be a consulting service, which could serve as an effective way to jumpstart your business.

The Reality of Business Failure

Regrettably, a substantial number of new businesses don't survive past the first few years, often due to a lack of a business plan, cash flow issues, or a misunderstanding of business principles.

These challenges highlight the importance of recognizing that a business only truly exists when it has paying customers. Your job is to identify those individuals who are likely to become your customers. Often, the reasons your customers choose to buy from you may not align with what you initially thought would attract them.

For instance, if you decide to open a pizza restaurant, customers might not come solely for the pizza; they might have certain expectations of what a good pizza should be, and you fulfill those expectations. However, your customers might be more attracted to the quiet, romantic, or private dining areas and the overall ambiance, which enhances their dining experience.

Finding Your First Paying Customer

To secure your first paying customer, you might want to consider offering a simple service or product.

A consulting service could be a viable option, where you get paid to teach, consult, or demonstrate a task. Your expertise is your greatest asset in this scenario.

How will you achieve success?

The key to business success is a robust business plan, streamlined operations, and a comprehensive understanding of business principles. However, bear in mind that despite the most meticulous planning, customer requirements can differ significantly, necessitating your business to adapt and cater to their needs. Thus, your business plan should act as a roadmap to initiate your journey, helping you contemplate the processes and keep you on the right path. Nevertheless, be ready to modify your plan to accommodate the demands of your paying customers. Above all, never forget that your business exists to serve your customers. Hence, your primary objective should be to comprehend their needs, surpass their expectations, and forge enduring relationships with them. And always remember, anyone could be a potential customer. So, go out there and find them.

Rethinking the Route to Your First Customer

Many people believe that a product or service must be fully developed before acquiring the first customer, which can often lead to a vicious cycle of failure. This perspective might not always be accurate. Some business models require substantial capital to launch and are not considered in this book. Starting a business that requires significant investment when you're financially constrained can be a daunting task. Borrowing might seem like a viable option, but it often comes with conditions that might leave you as an employee or partner rather than the owner. This book is not intended for individuals in such situations.

Debt-free Business and Customer as a Capital Source

This book is aimed at those with limited investment resources and a reluctance to accrue debt. The drawbacks of debt in business are manifold; if the business stumbles, stagnates, or ceases, repaying the debt becomes an overwhelming challenge. The suggested approach here is to identify a customer, finalize a sale, and secure payment. In this way, your customer becomes your source of operating capital, saving you from debt and assisting you in building capital. While this may seem overly simplistic, it is a strategy with significant merit and has been the foundation for numerous businesses.

Identifying Your Customer

Customers are individuals seeking a solution to a problem. Your objective is to demonstrate your ability to solve their problem and charge for your service. This is a well-established business practice. Many potential customers are keen to resolve their issues and are willing to pay in advance, either in full or partially. In the digital world, advance payment is more the norm than the exception.

Focusing on Potential Customers

Identifying your potential customers necessitates understanding who they are, and equally importantly, who they are not. By excluding certain market segments, you can hone your focus, saving time and increasing your chances of securing paying customers.

Avoiding Cash Flow Problems

Cash flow difficulties are often the most pressing concern for startups. The allure to use credit cards or bank loans can be irresistible, but this can create more problems than it solves. These resources can quickly deplete and require repayment. The optimal cash flow strategy is to avoid spending money that you don't have. The most effective way to prevent cash flow issues is to secure paying customers. Make it a practice to ask for payment before, during, or after the delivery of your service or product.

Turning Theory into Practice

The guidance I'm providing isn't just theoretical; it's based on my personal experiences. I'm not a journalist or a reporter, but I've learned from my own business ventures. I've found that openly discussing your startup's status and asking for payment for your problem-solving services can be very effective. The pricing should already be agreed upon; the conversation at this stage is about when payment will be made.

The Confidence of Winning Your First Customer

Landing your first customer can be a game-changer. It's a clear indication of success and growth. Picturing this outcome can help you get ready for any objections or negativity, and build the confidence needed to win your first customer. This isn't just a mental exercise, but a way to adopt a successful mindset. However, imagination alone won't do the trick; you still need to persuade a customer to purchase your product or service.

The True Reward of Winning Your First Customer

The benefit of securing your first customer extends beyond just financial gain. While money is certainly crucial, the greater reward is the sense of pride and the confidence boost you'll feel. This accomplishment proves that your goals are achievable and provides you with the know-how to repeat the process.

The Safety in Starting Business Without Money

Arguably, the safest way to start a business is without any initial investment, as it creates a situation where you have everything to gain and nothing to lose. The main objective of a business is to make money. If you invest your own money, especially at the beginning, you risk losing it. Therefore, acquiring customers first isn't just a cost-saving strategy; it's also about reducing risk.

Investment Timing and Growth Strategy

Investment should be considered when your business starts to generate a consistent cash flow. The money you earn from your business should be what you use to expand it. However, growth should only be pursued once you've confirmed your business's viability and feel comfortable moving forward.

Understanding That Practice Makes Perfect

Your first business venture doesn't have to be flawless. Perfection comes with practice, a universally accepted truth. Some people invest in businesses that align with their dreams, only to realize that the reality doesn't match their expectations. For example, during lockdown, many city dwellers heavily invested in rural farms, dreaming of a peaceful countryside life. However, many of them soon realized that farm life wasn't for them and yearned to return to the city.

Enhancing Your Business Acumen

This book's purpose is to provide you with the essential skills needed to ensure your business thrives. Should you find yourself needing additional funds, these skills will direct you back to your customer base, your primary source of revenue. The concept of learning how to fish, so you can always go back to the water for nourishment, is fundamental to the philosophy of starting a business without any capital.

Establishing a Robust Business Foundation

If you're contemplating a startup or have recently launched a business, there are crucial factors to consider. Having collaborated with thousands of entrepreneurs worldwide across various industries, I've heard numerous inspiring goals and seen many successes. I've observed that those who achieve success are true scholars of their craft, dedicating time to thoroughly contemplate every facet of their business.

However, the distinction between success and failure often boils down to whether or not one prioritizes customer needs. Putting customers first means not focusing on expenditures such as equipment, leases, capital investments, hiring staff, securing a location, and so on.

One of the most prevalent family investments before the pandemic was in the restaurant industry. Families would pool resources to secure a lease or purchase a property, then outfit it with state-of-the-art kitchen equipment. Organizing this requires a significant amount of time and effort, all without truly understanding the customer's desires.

Auctions are an excellent place to find affordable kitchen equipment, primarily because most restaurants fail.

How to start your business

Often, people believe that the first step to starting a business is raising capital or acquiring certain qualifications. While these steps can be beneficial, they are not necessarily the starting point. The primary focus should always be on the needs of the customer.

The first step is to identify a customer

Start by finding someone who requires your services and assist them. For instance, if you are a chef, cook delicious meals and look for a customer who is willing to pay for your culinary skills. Do you need a luxurious restaurant before securing your first customer? While location and ambiance can contribute to your business, it's not necessary to lease or purchase property right away. There are customers who would pay for a chef to come to their home, or people who would pay for cooking lessons. When starting, consider low-cost and quick methods to generate income. Offer your services to potential customers at a discounted rate. The fastest way to start a business is simply to begin. You need to assist customers who know what they want, even if you think you know their desires.

Business ideas evolve over time to cater to customer needs, so be prepared for change from the onset. Think about what adjustments you can make to appear more appealing and adaptable to potential customers.

For instance, there are successful 'flying' chefs who travel to customers' homes to prepare high-quality meals. Especially for those hosting guests, the chef becomes the star of the evening.

The second step is to maintain transparency with your customer

Be honest with your potential customers about your capabilities and limitations. If they still want to work with you after understanding the terms, that's great. Avoid making promises you can't keep. Instead, aim to exceed expectations. This will help build your reputation and attract referrals. In the early stages, case studies are essential to prove your capabilities to others.

The third step is to establish your terms

This is an extension of maintaining transparency with your customer, particularly regarding payment. You want customers who are willing to pay for your services. There are various ways to approach this. You could require a deposit, charge for expenses, or ask for payment in advance.

You can set a fixed fee for the entire job or charge an hourly or daily rate. It's your choice. You can also set a minimum or maximum in terms of hours or rate of pay. You negotiate and agree on a deal with a potential customer, informing them of the payment requirements. If an upfront payment is required, do not start the job until they have agreed to pay in advance.

It's advisable to have your customer's agreement in writing. For example, in a restaurant, the prices and food items are usually listed on a menu. Customers can see what they need to pay in advance, in writing.

Don't hesitate to ask for the order to proceed. In a restaurant, orders are typically taken by a waiter in writing. The waiter confirms the order before sending it to the kitchen. In other businesses, you might have a discussion and then confirm the agreement via email. This forms the basis for the work you will carry out.

As your business grows, you can publish terms and conditions on your website and prepare contracts for clients to sign. You can also request purchase orders. Established businesses follow these practices, and you can too if you wish.

These three steps are crucial when starting a business. They may cause you to revise your ideas and processes. Always remember, most customers prefer a service that is tailored to their needs.

Avoid Offering Services for Free

Offering services for free to potential clients might seem like a good idea, but it can be costly and unwise. Many people consider giving a free sample of their work, such as new authors giving away their books. However, this could attract customers who never intend to pay. Furthermore, without a charge, there might not be a clear agreement about what is expected, leading to endless requests from the 'customer'. I learned this the hard way when I first started.

Also, if you don't value your work enough to charge for it, why should a potential client? A red flag is when a potential client insists that your first piece of work should be free, arguing that they don't know you or your capabilities.

If you feel compelled to accommodate them, consider offering a one-hour consultation, a first meeting, or some advice that could benefit them. Make it clear that if they want more, they will have to pay for your time or service.

Should You Offer Free Services?

If offering a free service can demonstrate your capabilities to potential clients, then it might be worth considering. Many professionals offer their first hour for free to understand the client's needs and establish a relationship. This also encourages the client to come to you, saving you time and money, and they might be more inclined to proceed having made the effort to visit.

An initial meeting or call can go in several directions. It can reveal a need that wasn't apparent initially, which could be beneficial for both parties. The meeting might excite you about the potential work, or it might make you realize it's not worth pursuing.

Ideally, an initial meeting could lead to a long-term business relationship. Alternatively, you might refer the potential client to another provider who might be a better fit.

Free Information

Free information can be provided in various formats, such as a downloadable guide, interactive chart, poster, audio file, or video. This information is typically focused on a specific aspect or problem and can help qualify potential clients based on their interests.

From the client's perspective, they're looking for a solution to their problem. If you appear to have the solution, they might choose you as their provider. Simply providing good information can form the basis of a great relationship and lead to bigger opportunities.

From your perspective as a provider, the free information might be the same information you would provide during an initial meeting. Therefore, offering free information online could save you time and effort, and once it's developed, the cost of providing it could be minimal.

As a provider, you should focus on the design and delivery of your information. It should be easily understood and contain an offer. Use simple language and avoid technical jargon if possible. The goal is to impress the client by providing information in a friendly, accessible, and straightforward manner. Ideally, your information should include an irresistible offer.

Free Services

While it's generally not advisable to offer your services for free, there are exceptions, especially when it comes to bulk deals. For instance, a "buy one, get one free" offer essentially provides a free item, contingent on a purchase. Similarly, you could offer a discount, such as 50% off, with the exact percentage varying based on your specific situation.

Gift Vouchers

Offering redeemable gift vouchers can be a great strategy. These are typically paper certificates with a monetary value that can only be redeemed at your business. They can be used in various ways, such as a thank you for patronage, a reward for referrals, or both. The goal is to encourage recipients to spend their vouchers. This strategy works well in networking, retail, and event settings.

Newsletters and Magazines

Regularly providing clients with information can be an effective way to stay connected and showcase your relevance to keep their interest. Customers often choose your services because they align with their values and needs. They appreciate that you can perform tasks they require without them needing to develop internal expertise, saving them time and potentially reducing costs.

Newsletters or magazines are usually concise yet impactful, highlighting topics within your field of expertise that are significant to your clients. This not only shows your ongoing commitment but also reminds your customers why they choose to do business with you.

Many businesses now distribute newsletters or magazines electronically. While this may be cheaper, fewer people are likely to read them as they can easily get lost among numerous other emails. Instead, consider printing and mailing hard copies. This extra effort is likely to yield positive results.

Moreover, having your own publication can help maintain social connections with customers. Newsletters can be used to celebrate social events and even invite people to birthdays, trips, or other gatherings. They often include additional entertainment, such as puzzles and jokes. There are plenty of software options available to assist in creating these publications.

Content Strategy Continuation

In layman's terms, generating one article per week could be sufficient to fill a newsletter or provide a continuous stream of free information. Each article can be posted on your website to enhance your SEO. The weekly creation of articles allows you to engage with current affairs by commenting on recent news reports. You can reference the source and reiterate important details, ensuring not to copy the original article verbatim. Your task is to provide your personal interpretation of the story or explain how the recent events could be beneficial.

There are always new developments. Frequently, you'll discover relevant stories in business sections or even on Google for you to analyze. References to these stories and events can be included in your newsletters and magazines.

Significant events are reported in newspapers daily. It's entirely possible to connect your interests, skills, and accomplishments to an ongoing issue like climate change. For instance, it's reported that CNN will be concentrating on climate change for the foreseeable future, with other broadcasters likely to follow suit. While this may seem cynical, it's also popular, as many of us are interested in learning more about it.

Climate change has been a growing concern since the 1800s. It's a long-standing issue that tugs at our existential fears and impacts everyone. There's plenty of opportunity for us all to contribute to the efforts to stop our planet's decline.

Every day, numerous other stories are reported in the news that may be more relevant to attracting your future customers. There are countless reasons to start a business, and any event could spark your desire to do so.

Many of us have interests, hobbies, or professions that others might share. This alone could be a good reason to start a business. For example, my first legitimate business was born out of a home computer hobby I had as a youngster. In a short amount of time, it turned out to be quite profitable. Here's a brief story: After a conversation with a dentist, I discovered how to assist other dentists in transitioning from patient care to practice management. I didn't need any knowledge of dentistry to advise dentists and get paid for my time.

A seasoned dentist can easily assist other practitioners because they have decades of experience in dentistry. It's a common trajectory, but many don't see the obvious opportunity to mentor others when they have industry experience.

Even without any subject matter expertise, it's possible to advise those who do. You don't need any experience to start a business. What you do need is a customer. Whether you offer advice, dig holes, stack shelves, or deliver goods, someone will compensate you. The possibilities are endless.

Start soon

When launching a business, many individuals tend to spend money on unnecessary items. Do you really need business cards, a new phone, an office, a car, or a photocopier? These items often come with a monthly financial commitment. While you might be able to afford the initial payments, the challenge lies in maintaining them. You need a consistent monthly income to cover these costs, or else your business could end up in chaos.

So, who are you really working for? Yourself or the finance companies?

The perceived cost of doing business often deters people. However, you don't need most of these expenses, at least not in the beginning. You can rent an office by the hour, pay for photocopies as needed, use Uber for transportation, hire a virtual assistant for specific tasks, and get a business card designed on fiverr.com, among other things.

My first business venture began with a borrowed bucket and sponge. As a teenager, I used these items to find customers just a few doors down. The point is, you don't need to borrow money; you can borrow whatever you need to get started without spending a dime.

It's possible to start from nothing and eventually consult with major brands and household names. I did it. I started from scratch. The only thing I felt I needed to purchase was a suit.

If a business is indeed a business, it will generate money. Therefore, the true test of a business is whether it makes money. If you can't figure out what to charge for, you don't have a business yet.

Don't get discouraged; Rome wasn't built in a day. You'll figure it out and eventually find yourself running a business.

There's a right time and place to invest money in a business, and the first investment should ideally be directed towards generating profits. We often invest money in a business hoping for a return on investment, but what if the business fails? How much should we invest or risk? The concept of a no-money-down business is to eliminate the initial risk by not investing any money upfront.

By doing this, you can be much more flexible.

If we invest money into something, we tend to focus all our energy on recouping that investment. But what if our potential customers aren't interested in what we're selling, which is often the case? Then what?

Learning Through Investment

Family-owned restaurants are a common sight due to the universal love for food and the joy derived from sharing culinary creations. It's not unusual to see extended family members pooling resources to start a restaurant, only for it to fail eventually.

The restaurant business demands significant capital for various reasons, including long-term rental agreements, kitchen setup, perishable inventory, and dining area furnishings. These factors are potential pitfalls. Regardless of customer traffic, expenses such as staff wages, rent, and taxes persist daily, monthly, and annually. The constant costs can quickly become overwhelming, making the restaurant business a challenging one. Kudos to every family that successfully manages a restaurant despite these hurdles.

Business failures are often termed as 'paid for learning.' If you have a steady income, you might be able to afford these expensive lessons. I've had my fair share of such experiences. It's an unfortunate reality that even the best aren't immune to. Starting a business this way is tough because you not only have to recover your initial investment but also generate profit. Why complicate things unnecessarily?

In my experience, the most successful ventures required no initial capital. That said, reinvesting profits to expand the business and boost sales and growth can be beneficial. Banks are even willing to lend money to finance confirmed orders.

However, taking financial risks to grow a business from scratch shouldn't be necessary. If your idea is good, customers will pay for it. It's as simple as that.

Another common mistake is the notion of starting an 'internet business.' This perspective is flawed because the internet isn't a customer; it doesn't purchase anything.

You should begin by identifying how you can serve customers. The internet is merely a medium that delivers messages. It's the customers who dictate what those messages should be.

Once you've identified your target audience, find out which media they frequently use. If they're accessible via the internet, that's great. However, avoid becoming one of those entrepreneurs who've lost everything on the internet due to a misguided business approach.

If you take the time to read the next chapter, you might find yourself operating a small business and generating income quickly. All it takes is the implementation of a few ideas that you'll discover there.

CHAPTER 2: GENERATING BUSINESS CONCEPTS

Wondering where to begin with your business idea? How does it function? How can you apply it to the business you're considering? Allow me to explain: the genesis of a business idea comes after you've determined what you want to pursue.

Starting a business requires considerable effort, including the development of a business plan, attracting investors, securing funding, and hiring personnel. However, before you can embark on these steps, you need a solid business idea. Regardless of how innovative or unique your product or service may be, it must be something that customers need and are willing to pay for. To come up with a great idea, you need to engage in thoughtful reflection, tap into your creativity, and conduct thorough research. Here are some things to keep in mind when trying to generate business ideas for your own startup.

How to Generate Ideas

Think about the products and services that could improve your life. Make a list of your unique skills and areas that could use some improvement. From that list, identify any potential solutions that could enhance your quality of life. Reflect on your personal experiences and take the time to analyze them. With enough thought and effort, you can certainly come up with a variety of useful products or services.

Decide if you want to offer a product or a service. The basis of a new business idea usually revolves around either a product or a service. Each option requires careful consideration and creativity. Before choosing one over the other, weigh the pros and cons of each:

• If you plan to sell a product, it needs to be developed or enhanced before you can invest in production. Creating and manufacturing new products can be expensive, but it can also be very profitable if successful.

• On the other hand, if you choose to offer a service, you won't need to worry about product creation and manufacturing. However, relying solely on providing a service can make it difficult to scale your business, as you may need to hire more staff. Regardless of the route you choose, investing time and resources in marketing and promotion is essential.

Identify a problem in a market segment that you're familiar with. Have you recently bought a product that you think could be better in terms of quality? Were you unhappy with a certain service? Sometimes, dissatisfaction with current offerings can inspire you to start a business or create something new. Keep an eye out for such issues as they come up, as they may point to a market need that you can meet. For instance, if there are no bike repair services in your community, you've identified a gap in the market that you can fill by offering that service.

Consider enhancing an existing business concept. Instead of solely trying to solve industry issues, you can also learn from successful companies. Examine if you can refine an established idea and create your unique market segment. Google exemplifies this method, as it transformed the internet search engine industry by creating a highly precise algorithm for better search results. Numerous prosperous companies and entrepreneurs have begun by improving existing products or services. You can also adopt this approach.

Think about future trends. Successful entrepreneurs are visionary and foresee emerging opportunities. By observing current trends and predicting their natural progression, you can come up with unique ideas that may disrupt the market. For example, with the growing popularity of remote teaching, starting a company that provides tools to support remote teachers could be a game-changing idea. Analyzing current trends and advancing them can reveal untapped potential.

Carry out initial consumer research. Although market research is usually done post-ideation, conducting preliminary studies can help align your ideas with consumer needs and wants. Discover what people are looking for by carrying out online research. Use search engine tools like Bing Ads or Google AdWords to identify trending keywords. Also, consider engaging directly with potential customers through face-to-face interviews or online surveys to understand their preferences better.

Use your expertise in a different sector. Another way to create new products or services is to utilize the skills you've gained from previous experiences. Applying your expertise creatively in unrelated industries can often lead to breakthroughs. For example, Leo Fender, who started as a radio repairman, used his knowledge of electronics and engineering to revolutionize the music industry. By applying his expertise to guitar design and manufacturing, he created iconic instruments that forever altered how musicians play and express themselves. This example illustrates the power of using your existing skills and knowledge in a different field to generate innovative business ideas.

To illustrate this idea further, think about delving into sectors that are not directly related to your area of specialization. Seek out ways to apply your unique skills and viewpoints to different fields. For example, if you're a software developer, you could use your coding skills to devise innovative solutions for the healthcare or finance sectors. By thinking creatively and adopting interdisciplinary methods, you can uncover untapped opportunities and introduce groundbreaking ideas.

In addition, collaborating and networking can boost the creation of business ideas. Connect with professionals from various fields, attend industry events and workshops, and join online groups that align with your interests. By exposing yourself to a variety of knowledge sources, you can gain insights from different viewpoints and identify potential collaborations and partnerships that stimulate innovative thinking.

Keep in mind, the process of creating business ideas isn't limited to a single flash of inspiration. It's a continuous journey of discovery, investigation, and fine-tuning. Be receptive to feedback and constantly improve your ideas. Adopt the attitude of a lifelong student, and let your experiences and interactions with the world influence and develop your entrepreneurial vision.

By actively participating in the process of creating business ideas, you can uncover unique opportunities, devise valuable solutions, and make a significant impact. The journey to success starts with the spark of an idea and the resolve to make it a reality. Embrace your passion, utilize your expertise, and embark on this thrilling entrepreneurial journey.

Remember, the world is eager for your innovative ideas. Let your entrepreneurial spirit fly high, and together, we can shape a more promising future.

UNCOVERING IDEAS

Think about the products and services that could improve your life. Make a list of your unique talents and areas where you need more knowledge. Look at this list and see if any of these items could enhance your life. Spend time reflecting on your personal experiences. By dedicating time and thought, you will undoubtedly come up with a variety of useful products or services.

Decide if you want to offer a product or a service. The basis of a new business idea usually revolves around two options: a product or a service. Each choice requires careful thought and creativity. Before choosing one over the other, consider the pros and cons of each:

- If you're thinking about a product-based business, consider the need to create or improve the product if it already exists in the market.

- Offering a service eliminates the need for product creation and manufacturing.

- While developing new products can be expensive, successful ones can be highly profitable.

- However, if you only offer a service, growing your business may be difficult, requiring the hiring of additional staff. Regardless of the strategy you choose, investing time and resources in marketing and promotion is crucial.

Identify a problem in a market segment you are familiar with. Have you recently bought a product and were disappointed with its quality? Were you unhappy with a certain service? Sometimes, being unhappy with existing methods inspires people to start a business or create something new. Actively look for such problems to come up with business ideas. It's possible that others share your dissatisfaction, creating a market opportunity. For example, if there is no bike repair service in your community, recognizing this unmet need gives you the opportunity to provide that service.

Adapt an existing business idea. Instead of focusing on shortcomings in the current industry, you can look at companies that are doing well. Find ways to improve their methods. By taking an existing idea and pushing it further than competitors, you can create a unique place in the market. Google is a great example of improving on an already successful idea. When Google came out, there were several other search engines. However, Google's accurate algorithm greatly improved search results, leading to its incredible success. Many other successful companies or business owners have followed a similar path by improving existing products or services. You can do this too.

Think about future trends. Successful entrepreneurs are visionaries who anticipate future changes and use them to their advantage, rather than sticking to outdated methods or technologies. This could involve predicting the logical progression of a product line or expanding services. By looking at current trends and pushing them forward, you can come up with a unique idea that could potentially transform the market. For example, with the increasing popularity of distance learning, you could consider starting a company specializing in tools to help remote teachers. Come up with an idea that is innovative and has the potential to reshape the industry.

Do initial consumer research. While market research is usually done after coming up with an idea, you can still gather initial insights into what consumers want. This will help you shape your idea based on the needs and wants of potential customers. Do online research to find frequently searched keywords, as these can provide inspiration. Alternatively, services like Bing Ads or Google AdWords can provide more detailed data on popular search terms.

Use your skills in a different field. Another way to come up with new services is to use your skills and expertise from a different field. Think about the knowledge and skills you have and see how they could be used in a different industry or context. This approach allows you to bring a new perspective and unique solutions to an existing market.

Engage in collective brainstorming. Working together with others can be an effective strategy in producing business ideas. Initiate conversations with friends, coworkers, or mentors who possess knowledge in entrepreneurship or various fields. Their advice and viewpoints can ignite fresh ideas and assist you in refining your plans.

Stay updated on new technologies or sectors. Pay attention to new technologies, sectors, or societal shifts that could potentially disrupt current markets or generate new prospects. Keep yourself updated about progress in areas like artificial intelligence, blockchain, renewable energy, or biotechnology, and think about how you can utilize these advancements to develop innovative goods or services.

Focus on specific markets. Instead of aiming for wide markets, think about concentrating on specific markets with distinct needs and preferences. Recognize underserved or neglected customer groups with unique needs. By serving these specialized markets, you can set yourself apart from the competition and establish a dedicated customer base.

Learn from successful business models. Analyze successful business models from various sectors and pinpoint crucial elements that contribute to their success. Search for patterns, innovative strategies, or gaps in their services that you can incorporate into your own business idea. This can offer valuable insights and motivation for creating your own distinctive concept.

Evaluate your ideas. After you've compiled a list of potential business ideas, it's crucial to evaluate them before investing substantial resources. Carry out market research, collect feedback from potential clients, and evaluate the feasibility and viability of each idea. This evaluation process will assist you in identifying the most promising ideas and making informed choices about which ones to follow.

Creating a successful business concept necessitates a blend of creativity, market awareness, and research. By taking into account your own abilities and experiences, identifying market gaps or issues, modifying existing ideas, predicting future trends, collaborating with others, and staying updated on new technologies, you can produce innovative and feasible business ideas. Always remember to evaluate your ideas before proceeding, as this will enhance your likelihood of establishing a successful and sustainable business.

CHAPTER 3: THE BEST BUSINESS MODEL CRITERIA

Many business owners struggle to find success, with numerous ventures hovering on the brink of collapse. However, a handful of businesses not only manage to stay afloat but also prosper for extended periods, consistently yielding considerable profits. What differentiates these successful businesses from the rest? The key lies in their foundation - their business models.

In this chapter, we delve into the art of designing profitable business models, the bedrock of lasting success. We will pinpoint the essential traits that set successful ventures apart from short-lived ones. Whether you're an entrepreneur, a business owner, or someone considering the entrepreneurial path, understanding the principles behind these extraordinary models can offer you a roadmap to success in your venture.

By exploring the key takeaways, you will gain insights that challenge traditional views on entrepreneurship. From the critical role of Lifetime Client Value (LCV) in generating sustainable revenue to the importance of securing external capital, each takeaway is a valuable nugget of information that sheds light on a vital aspect of building a profitable business.

As we examine the various traits that constitute a successful business model, you will discover the subtleties of predictable cash flow, the strength of niche specialization, the appeal of high entry barriers, and the potential for scalability. With real-life examples and practical insights, this chapter provides you with the tools to evaluate and select the right business model for you, guiding you towards a path of wealth.

Regardless of whether you're an experienced entrepreneur looking to fine-tune your business strategy or a budding innovator taking your initial steps in the entrepreneurial world, the lessons contained in this chapter are universally relevant. Here are some ideas to establish a foundation for sustainable growth, lasting value, and ultimately, a journey towards success that defies the odds.

1. The Significance of Choosing the Right Business Model:

A business model is akin to a roadmap that guides a venture towards success. It outlines how a business generates, delivers, and captures value. The selection of an appropriate model is crucial as it shapes the course of your business. A well-structured model harmoniously aligns your resources, target customer segments, and revenue channels, thereby promoting stability and growth.

2. The Emphasis on Lifetime Client Value (LCV):

The Lifetime Client Value is the cumulative value of a customer to your business throughout the entire relationship. Firms that underscore LCV prioritize fostering enduring relationships, often via subscription models or long-term contracts. This approach yields steady cash flow and improved customer retention rates, reducing the necessity for continuous customer acquisition.

3. The Need for Predictable Cash Flow and Revenue Streams:

Predictability is a coveted characteristic in business. Models that provide recurring services, subscriptions, or long-term contracts guarantee a stable cash flow. This financial stability acts as a safety net against market volatilities, facilitating better financial planning and resource distribution.

4. The Attraction of Investor and Fund Interest:

Interest from investors and funds in a business model is an indicator of its potential for growth and profitability. A robust model lures external capital, expediting expansion and boosting credibility. Investors appreciate the promise of steady cash flows and the prospect of predictable returns.

5. The Advantage of a High Barrier to Entry:

A high entry barrier prevents competitors from easily duplicating your business. Models with unique value offerings, proprietary technology, or specialized knowledge build protective moats around the business, enabling you to demand higher prices and sustain profitability.

6. The Benefit of Niche Focus and Specialization:

Niche businesses serve a specific market segment, establishing profound connections with their audience. Specialization facilitates the creation of customized products or services that strongly resonate with customers, leading to brand loyalty and diminished competition.

7. The Impact of Regulation and Standardization:

Business models functioning within regulated industries enjoy the advantage of a uniform competitive environment. Regulations establish guidelines that all competitors must adhere to, reducing market volatility and ensuring stability. This factor can foster a conducive environment for continuous profitability.

8. The Importance of Scalability and Exit Strategy:

Scalability refers to a model's capacity to expand without a proportional increase in costs. A scalable model attracts investors and prepares the business for mergers, acquisitions, or public offerings. The possibility of an exit strategy enhances the model's attractiveness.

9. The Strategy of Diversification and Portfolio Approach:

By operating multiple profitable business models, diversification reduces risks associated with market fluctuations. A combination of models with diverse customer bases, revenue channels, and industries can result in a more robust business portfolio.

10. The Vision of Long-Term Sustainability and Growth:

Profitable business models are designed for longevity. Their emphasis on stable revenue channels and enduring customer relationships aligns with sustainable growth. Such models are resilient to economic downturns and set businesses up for long-term success.

11. The Necessity of Research and Due Diligence:

Comprehensive research is crucial before settling on a business model. It's important to understand the market, competitors, customer requirements, and regulatory landscape. Due diligence helps minimize risks and ensures you're entering a market with growth potential. Continuous research, which is a tax-deductible expense, can help the business stay competitive.

12. The Need for Adaptation and Innovation:

Business environments are dynamic, requiring flexibility and innovation. Even with a profitable model, continuous adaptation to shifting customer preferences, technological advancements, and market trends is essential to maintain relevance and success.

As you navigate through these key insights, bear in mind that they are interlinked. Constructing a profitable business model involves understanding and integrating multiple aspects to formulate a comprehensive strategy that promotes long-term success.

40 businesses that share some or all the business models

It's important to bear in mind that not all companies will perfectly match every characteristic, and each business model's success can depend on a variety of factors. Some of these businesses may need a little financial boost to start, but in most cases, they require seed capital for initial rents and deposits, not large capital investments. Starting these businesses may require some labor, meaning you might have to do some work yourself or seek help from friends and family. However, due to their inherent characteristics, each of these businesses is likely to be sustainable and carry minimal risk.

1. Day Nurseries:

Operating day nurseries for children can provide a good average lifetime value as customers usually stay for several years. This business model also involves upfront payment for services, ensuring a steady cash flow. It's regulated by the government, which standardizes competition. Furthermore, the author notes that external funding sources (investors, banks, etc.) are interested in this sector, making it a potentially profitable model.

2. Private Preschools/Kindergartens:

Similar to day nurseries, private preschools provide a stable income due to long-term students and upfront payments.

3. Food Services Business:

Offering food services to large groups such as offices, factories, and schools guarantees regular and repeat customers, leading to a predictable cash flow. This stability makes it an appealing model. Additionally, the author points out that investors and funds are interested in this sector, indicating its potential profitability.

4. Event Catering Companies:

Event catering services, which operate on contracts, offer consistent business from clients who require catering for their events.

5. Contract Catering:

Like food services, contract catering involves supplying food to schools, factories, or office blocks on a contract basis. This provides even more predictable revenue since the customer base is well-defined and contracts are usually long-term. The fact that major players are investing in this sector adds to its viability.

6. Commercial Property Rentals:

Investing in commercial properties and leasing them out can yield stable rental income, especially if the property is also your business location. This model benefits from tax efficiencies and can be relatively resistant to economic downturns. Commercial property rentals offer long-term stability and income potential.

7. Shared Office Space:

Leasing office spaces to multiple businesses provides a steady income stream from long-term contracts.

8. Commercial Storage Facilities:

Offering storage solutions to businesses can lead to recurring revenue and long-term contracts.

9. Commercial Hygiene and Waste Services:

Providing services like waste disposal and hygiene services to commercial entities ensures steady demand and revenue. The author emphasizes that these businesses tend to be recession-proof and can attract investment interest due to their predictable nature.

10. Commercial Cleaning Services:

Similar to hygiene and waste services, cleaning services offer recurring contracts for maintaining cleanliness in commercial spaces.

11. Medical Professionals (Dentists, Doctors):

These professionals maintain long-lasting relationships with their patients, leading to high lifetime client values due to repeat appointments and continued care.

12. Law Firms:

Law firms, similar to medical practices, have high client values due to the ongoing legal requirements and sustained partnerships.

13. Accounting Companies:

Accounting firms provide continuous value through regular financial management and tax assistance, similar to law firms.

14. Financial Advisory Services:

These services, which include financial advice and planning, can result in long-term client relationships and high lifetime values.

15. Commercial Property Owners:

Owners of commercial properties can earn steady rental income from long-term lease agreements.

16. Physical Therapy Clinics:

Physical therapy clinics, like medical practices, provide ongoing services and maintain long-term relationships with patients.

17. HR Consultancy Firms:

These firms offer human resources consulting services to businesses, which involves long-term relationships and contract-based work.

18. Veterinary Clinics:

Veterinary clinics provide long-term client relationships and repeat visits for pet care, similar to medical practices.

19. Educational Tutoring Services:

Tutoring services can lead to long-term relationships with both students and their parents.

20. Fitness Centers:

Fitness centers can generate predictable income from regular attendees through memberships and class packages.

21. Subscription Box Companies:

These companies offer niche products through subscriptions, creating recurring revenue from loyal customers.

22. Commercial Landscaping Services:

These services provide landscaping and outdoor maintenance to businesses, involving recurring contracts for ongoing services.

23. Commercial Waste Management:

Like hygiene services, waste management companies generate predictable income from contracted services.

24. Printing and Signage Companies:

These companies can establish long-term relationships with businesses for their branding needs.

25. Childcare Franchise:

Operating a childcare center franchise offers a proven business model with a high potential for profit.

26. Elderly Home Care Services:

Long-term client relationships and regular services are a part of providing home care services to the elderly.

27. Language Academies:

Continuous relationships with students can be formed by providing language learning courses.

28. Fitness Gear Rental Services:

A steady income can be generated by leasing fitness equipment to businesses or individuals.

29. Corporate Training Courses:

Long-term partnerships with companies seeking professional growth are part of providing corporate training courses.

30. IT Assistance Services:

Ongoing tech support contracts with businesses can be secured by providing IT assistance.

31. Commercial Pest Management Services:

Pest control firms can establish ongoing contracts to ensure a pest-free environment.

32. Architectural Companies:

Long-term projects and client relationships are involved in providing design and planning services.

33. Commercial Real Estate Agencies:

Substantial commissions and long-term clients can be earned by brokering commercial real estate transactions.

34. Business Mentoring/Advisory Services:

High-value, long-term relationships can be established by providing mentoring or advisory services to businesses.

35. Children's Enrichment Centers (Art, Music):

Long-term programs with regular attendance are offered at children's enrichment centers.

36. Corporate Health Programs:

Long-term contracts and recurring services are involved in offering wellness programs to corporations.

37. Corporate Event Management:

Contracts for coordinating various corporate events are provided by business event planning.

38. Executive Recruitment Agencies:

High-value contracts and long-term relationships can be secured by providing executive recruitment services.

39. Medical Invoicing Services:

Ongoing services and long-term contracts are involved in managing medical billing for healthcare providers.

40. Educational Publishing:

Consistent sales to schools and educational institutions can be achieved by producing educational materials.

CHAPTER 4: INITIATING A BUSINESS

Compiling your idea list

Even the smallest or seemingly insignificant thought can hold immense potential. Therefore, it's beneficial to make a habit of carrying an "idea notepad" where you can jot down any thoughts that come to mind, regardless of when they occur. Make sure this notepad is always within reach as you never know when a great idea might strike. This method allows you to gather all your ideas in one handy location. Make it a routine to go through this notepad to find any ideas that can be further developed or expanded.

You might want to consider transferring these ideas to a digital device like a computer or phone, depending on what's more convenient for you. However, having a physical notebook is always a good option. Having a digital backup ensures you don't lose your ideas if your notebook gets lost or damaged. Digital storage also allows you to organize and categorize your ideas more efficiently, which can enhance your creative thinking process. When brainstorming, avoid being too critical of your ideas. Give yourself the freedom to daydream and explore any thoughts that come up. Use different techniques to stimulate your imagination and encourage idea generation.

To increase your motivation and inspiration, incorporate regular walks into your routine. These walks are not only good for your health, but they can also stimulate your imagination. There is plenty of research that shows how walking can positively impact brain health, especially in relation to creativity. Bring your journal along on these walks to jot down any insights or ideas that come to mind. You can also find inspiration by visiting local stores, especially large department stores. Look around and make a list of the products and services you see. Think about how these items could be improved or fixed. Don't miss out on unseen opportunities as they can lead to potentially untapped yet commercially viable ideas.

Broaden your perspectives by interacting with people from various professions. If you're working on software development, for example, seek advice not just from IT experts but also from professionals in other fields. Try new experiences and engage with unfamiliar people. Observe how they use products or services to improve their lives. This approach can inspire you to come up with ideas from new perspectives and innovative angles.

Take short breaks to give your brain a chance to relax and generate ideas effortlessly. Many great ideas come to people when they're not actively trying to think of them. Take a break from intense thinking and focus on activities like reading, walking, watching a movie, or other enjoyable hobbies. Try not to think about your business, product, or service during this downtime. You might be surprised when the solution to a problem suddenly comes to you.

Getting enough sleep is crucial for keeping your brain sharp and alert. Make sure you prioritize a good night's sleep to optimize your brain's performance. Keep a pen and notepad near your bed in case any breakthroughs or original ideas come to you in your dreams.

EVALUATING YOUR SUGGESTIONS

Evaluate the pros and cons of your proposal. Even if your idea seems groundbreaking, it's important to assess if you have the necessary resources to bring it to life. For instance, the prospect of opening a restaurant may be enticing, but you need to consider whether you have the required experience or culinary training to make it successful.

Check if your idea is unique. It's quite possible that if an idea has occurred to you, someone else may have thought of something similar. Do some research to see if your business idea has already been implemented. You wouldn't want to invest a lot of time and effort into an idea only to find out later that it's already been executed. A comprehensive investigation is needed to ensure the originality of your idea.

Begin with an online search, using relevant keywords to find any existing solutions or ideas. If you don't find a perfect match, dig deeper to see if there are any businesses similar to yours. Bear in mind that this process can be time-consuming and complicated, and you might need to seek help from a patent law expert to navigate it successfully.

Analyze your competitors. If you discover that your idea has already been thought of, don't lose heart. Many new businesses face stiff competition initially, but they manage to overcome it by offering superior products or services. It's vital to thoroughly research potential competitors.

Interact with your competitors' customers through formal or informal surveys. Ask them about their satisfaction levels and areas of dissatisfaction, which will help you tweak your operations to address their concerns. Explore your competitors' online presence, including blogs and review websites, to identify any criticisms or weaknesses in their operations.

Before seeking customer feedback, share your idea with trusted friends, family, and colleagues. Explain to them how your idea could benefit the market and ask for their honest opinions and whether they would consider buying your product or service. Their initial evaluation can provide valuable insights, whether it's approval, constructive criticism, or feedback highlighting potential problems. Be open to all kinds of feedback.

Interact with potential customers to measure their interest in your idea. Once you have a concept that you believe in and have shared it with close friends, widen your scope to see if there's a market for your business. Try different methods to see if people would be interested in using your services.

Carry out in-person interviews with individuals who might be prospective customers. For instance, if you're designing a new fishing lure, engage with staff in the fishing department of various sports shops. Share your potential business concept and ask about their interest in that particular market segment. Make sure these discussions are brief to respect their time.

Think about sending out questionnaires via email using platforms like Google Forms. Distribute these surveys among your personal contacts, asking for their feedback, and encourage them to share them within their circles.

Recognize and assess potential risks and challenges linked to your plan. Every business venture comes with risks, whether they are financial or emotional. Predict hurdles and think about strategies to overcome them to enhance the chances of effectively handling potential threats and sustaining your business. Here are a few tips to tackle common hurdles:

Only partner with trustworthy individuals to prevent adverse effects on your business.

Always evaluate your financial resources before proceeding. Insufficient funds are a major reason for startup failure.

Be willing to adapt to market shifts to remain competitive.

View failure as a learning experience, and be ready to adjust and fine-tune your strategy.

Ensure your plan is practical and executable. Take into account various factors and ponder over them thoroughly before committing to your idea. Here are some points to consider:

Reflect on the outcomes of the surveys and interviews you've conducted. Does your idea have a market?

Be truthful with yourself and avoid optimistic bias if there's limited interest from potential customers.

Assess the competition level and devise a comprehensive strategy to outperform competitors.

Examine the costs related to your plan, including both startup and ongoing expenses. Evaluate the economic feasibility of your idea and assess your available financial resources.

Estimate the projected expenses and potential revenue linked to your plan.

Organize your concepts by ranking them from best to worst. After addressing the previous questions, assess the performance of each concept. Arrange them with the most promising one at the top. This ensures your efforts are concentrated on developing your strongest concept. Concepts at the bottom of the list should either be discarded or significantly enhanced before considering execution. To ensure the success of your shoe business, it's vital to accurately identify your target market. Assuming that every person on the street is a potential customer is unrealistic. Instead, concentrate on a smaller target market, such as middle-class teenagers. Start by finding out the percentage of children from middle-class families in your country, as this will give you insights into the potential customer base.

Next, consider the specific shoe needs of your target market. Investigate the types of shoes popular among middle-class teenagers. Are they interested in sports shoes, trendy sneakers, or formal footwear? Understanding their preferences will help you customize your product range to effectively meet their needs.

Assess the current market conditions to see if they are expanding or stagnant. Examine existing research on the footwear industry and conduct your own original study. This could involve interviews, customer surveys, or other data collection methods to gain important insights. Also, evaluate the competition in the market. Calculate the market share held by other footwear companies and identify how many competitors you will be up against.

To gain a competitive advantage, plan your strategies to distinguish yourself from other market participants. Evaluate the strengths and weaknesses of potential competitors and identify how your business can stand out. This evaluation will help you understand what makes your products or services unique and how they benefit your target customers. It's vital to clearly show how your customers will benefit from choosing your business over others.

Provide a detailed description of your product or service. Highlight the unique features and benefits that make your offerings attractive to customers. Start by outlining the problem your product or service solves and then explain your solution. Give an overview of how your product or service fits into the larger market context. Look at what solutions other companies are providing for this problem and emphasize what sets your offering apart.

In this section, detail every managerial and operational role within your business. Describe the organizational structure, remembering that it can be changed later. Assign roles and responsibilities to individuals or groups in charge of different business aspects. If you haven't hired staff yet, recognize the gaps and outline the tasks for those roles. Each team member should have a short profile highlighting relevant experience or qualifications that make them suitable for the role.

Create a detailed sales and marketing plan. Start by conducting an in-depth market study and defining your target buyer personas or ideal customers. Decide how you plan to enter the market and outline your strategies for business growth. Prioritize the most effective distribution channels and describe how you will interact with your customers.

Address questions about your sales strategy, expansion plans, sales team structure, average sale price, and the number of sales calls needed to close deals. Discuss your pricing strategy and provide a detailed financial plan, including estimated costs, funding needs, and projected revenue. If you're looking for investors, present your financial plan clearly, including start-up costs, cost forecasts, and a fundraising request.

By following these steps and using the advice provided, you can create a thorough business plan that covers all the key aspects of your footwear business and sets you up for success in the market.

To identify the initial costs of your business, you need to evaluate the projected expenses for the resources required to set up your enterprise, as well as the actual costs of obtaining these resources. Think about whether you need to rent office space or need a computer. It's essential to give accurate and reasonable estimates for these factors and their related costs to prevent running out of funds.

To gain funding for your enterprise, detail your costs and provide accurate financial projections to back them up. It's vital to ensure the precision of your financial model to increase your likelihood of securing funds from investors and lenders.

You might want to consider adding an appendix to your business plan. Although it's not compulsory, it's a good place to include relevant attachments such as rental contracts, permits or approvals, legal documents, cover letters, professional profiles of team members, and resumes of co-founders.

Choosing a name for your business is an important decision. This name will appear on official documents and in the business plan you present to investors. It's recommended to develop your strategy first before deciding on the name. Here are some strategies for naming your business:

Create a list of possible names: Use traditional brainstorming to come up with a variety of name options. For local businesses, adding the city name to the service provided can improve local search results. However, if your business is creative or unique, choose a distinctive and memorable name that fits your brand.

Perform a trademark search: Before settling on a name, conduct a trademark search to make sure it hasn't been registered or claimed by another business. Misusing a trademark can result in legal issues, so it's crucial to do your homework.

Verify name availability in your state: Check if the name you want is available and not already used by another company in your state. Business name registrations are usually specific to each state, but trademark problems can occur if the name is already trademarked.

Check domain name availability: Think about how the chosen name will look as a website domain. Make sure it's short, memorable, and easy to type. Check with domain name registrars to see if the domain name you want is available. Register the domain quickly to secure it.

If you've selected a unique name, you might want to register it as a trademark for added protection. Trademarks give owners exclusive rights to specific words, images, and logos related to their products and services.

Including the name of your business is optional and usually happens naturally during the registration process. However, if you operate under a name different from your registered name (relevant to sole proprietorships, partnerships, corporations, or existing LLCs), you may need to submit a "Doing Business As" (DBA) name application. The application process can be done at your state government or county clerk's office, depending on where you are located.

If you're uncertain about business structures like LLCs, corporations, or partnerships, don't stress. These are different types of legal entities that determine the hierarchical management of your company. We'll discuss how to choose the right structure later on.

SELECTING THE APPROPRIATE BUSINESS STRUCTURE

When launching a business, it's crucial to choose a legal structure that aligns with your needs, as it will affect your liabilities and tax obligations. The four primary business structures include a corporation, a limited liability company (LLC), a sole proprietorship, and a partnership. This guide will help you decide on the most suitable ownership structure:

SOLE PROPRIETORSHIP (SINGLE-OWNER BUSINESS) A sole proprietorship is a business owned and managed by one person. The owner and the business are not legally separate entities. Here are the advantages and disadvantages:

Advantages: Setting up a sole proprietorship is straightforward and inexpensive, and the owner has complete control over all business decisions. Tax filing is simpler as the owner's personal and business taxes are merged.

Disadvantages: The owner is personally responsible for all the business's risks and obligations. Raising capital or securing investors or loans can be difficult because the business doesn't have a separate legal entity.

Consider a sole proprietorship if you plan to be the only employee in the near future and are willing to bear the entire financial responsibility of the business.

PARTNERSHIP A partnership is a business model where two or more owners contribute to all aspects of the business and share its profits and losses. Here are the advantages and disadvantages:

Advantages: Establishing a partnership is relatively easy and less expensive. It allows for resource sharing and access to diverse skills and knowledge.

Disadvantages: Similar to a sole proprietorship, partners are personally liable for the business's risks and obligations. Conflicts between partners can occur, making it crucial to have a formal agreement.

Consider a partnership if you plan to start the business with another person and are comfortable sharing the liability and working in a collaborative manner.

LIMITED LIABILITY COMPANY (LLC) An LLC is a business model that provides limited liability protection to its owners while maintaining flexibility and simplicity. Here are the advantages and disadvantages:

Advantages: LLC owners have limited personal liability for the business's debts and obligations. It's easier to manage than a corporation with fewer formalities and regulations.

Disadvantages: Compared to sole proprietorships and partnerships, LLCs can have higher start-up costs. Some venture capital funds may be reluctant to invest in LLCs due to tax considerations and complexity.

Consider an LLC if you want limited liability protection and prefer a business model that is less complicated than a corporation.

CORPORATION A corporation is a separate legal entity from its owners, offering the most protection but also the most complexity. Here are the advantages and disadvantages:

Advantages: Owners' personal assets are safeguarded from the company's debts and liabilities. Corporations can easily attract venture capital and offer the best asset protection.

Disadvantages: Corporations have more complex tax and legal regulations, resulting in higher administrative costs. C corporations are subject to double taxation, and there are more formalities and regulations to adhere to.

Consider a corporation if you have secured enough venture capital or have a larger, more established business with multiple employees.

SETTING UP YOUR BUSINESS After deciding on the best ownership model, it's time to officially set up your business and meet all legal obligations. Here's what you need to do:

1. Choose your state of operation: Pick the state where your business will be based.

2. Register your business name: If you're setting up an LLC or sole proprietorship, your business name will be automatically registered. You might also want to think about a "Doing Business As" (DBA) name.

3. Get an Employer Identification Number (EIN): If you're not a sole proprietor or the only member of an LLC, you'll need to apply for an EIN from the IRS.

4. Meet any extra legal requirements: Depending on your industry and where you're based, you might need to get business licenses, permits, or certifications.

5. Understand your funding needs: Work out how much money you need to get your business off the ground and keep it running. Put together a detailed budget that includes all your costs, such as equipment, stock, marketing, and day-to-day operations.

6. Look at your personal resources: Think about using your own savings or personal assets to fund your business. This could mean dipping into your savings, using home equity, or selling non-essential personal assets.

7. Friends and family: Ask friends and family members if they'd be interested in investing in your business. Show them your business plan and financial forecasts to show them what kind of return they could expect on their investment.

8. Small business loans: Look into small business loans from banks, credit unions, or other financial institutions. Have a detailed business plan, financial statements, and collateral (if necessary) ready to support your loan application.

9. Government grants and programs: Look into government grants, subsidies, or programs that help small businesses. These can vary depending on where you're based and what industry you're in, so make sure you research options that are relevant to your business.

10. Venture capital and angel investors: If your business has a lot of growth potential and can be easily scaled up, you might want to think about getting investment from venture capitalists or angel investors. These investors give you money in return for shares in your company. Make sure you have a strong business pitch and try to meet potential investors at networking events or pitching competitions.

11. Crowdfunding: Look at crowdfunding platforms where people can donate money to help your business. Put together a strong

campaign that shows off your business idea, what makes it unique, and what people will get in return for their donation.

12. Strategic partnerships: Try to form strategic partnerships with established companies or organizations in your industry. They might be interested in giving you funding or resources in return for a mutually beneficial relationship.

13. Bootstrapping: Think about bootstrapping your business, which means funding it with your own revenue and profits. This approach requires a lean and frugal operation to generate enough cash flow to sustain and grow your business over time.

14. Remember, each funding option has its own advantages and considerations. Carefully evaluate the terms, potential impact on ownership and control, and repayment requirements before committing to any funding source. Additionally, consult with financial advisors or professionals to ensure you make informed decisions.

By choosing the right legal structure and funding strategy, you can build a solid foundation for your business's success.

CHAPTER 5: THE IMPORTANCE OF NO MONEY DOWN

Starting a business without any capital is a vastly different experience than starting one with funding. Having a surplus of working capital can sometimes lead to problems. If you begin with too much money, there's a higher chance that you might waste it, especially if you're investing in a personal idea. Such ideas are often driven by ego and the belief that with money, failure is impossible. All you need to do is implement your plans and manage the business effectively, ensuring it generates more income. The concept here is that money begets money.

Those who find themselves in this situation usually have a strong belief in their mission and are fully committed. This "go big or go home" mentality was prevalent during the dot-com boom, where every idea was considered a guaranteed success. Everyone seemed to be making a fortune, but this was mostly an illusion. Many were simply leveraging their family fortunes to cash in on the perceived dot-com boom.

The dot-com crash of 2001 resulted in nearly $8 trillion in losses. As a service business, we lost a few clients, but most of our clientele were banks and well-known retail and travel companies like Disney, which already had an online presence. Thankfully, we had a diverse range of clients and didn't lose many.

One particular business I won't name was a website based on a highly popular TV show at the time. The family behind the website was related to the TV producer and they were fully invested in the project. They had the advantage of using the show's design, branding, video clips, voices, and images. The TV show even promoted the website during its airtime. The website was perfectly set up for success, with thousands of daily sign-ups and high visitor traffic. It was the most popular website in its field.

Over the years, my agency's job was to drive more traffic to the site. We ensured it was search engine friendly and loaded quickly. The site was managed by a highly competent and dedicated team. It was number one in many related terms, making it an excellent case study.

However, there was one significant issue: the website wasn't making enough money. It turned out to be a financial black hole. The family had invested heavily in it, even going as far as re-mortgaging their house to raise funds.

They were always investing in the next big venture. They incorporated a high-end, fully-featured CRM with an integrated shopping cart, which did bring in a significant amount of revenue. However, I can't say for certain if they were making enough profit or getting a return on their investment because I didn't have access to their financial records. Despite this, the owners always reassured me that everything was going smoothly and they were excellent at settling their bills.

I genuinely enjoyed their company and they seemed to reciprocate the sentiment. They frequently invited me to their various product launches and even hired me to speak at their events to validate their traffic data. Every public appearance was a promotional opportunity. Those were good times. However, after several years, they announced that they were closing down.

It seems they couldn't make the business profitable. They quietly withdrew, likely cutting their losses. I believe they were people of integrity.

I attribute their downfall to their extravagant spending habits. They only bought the best and latest, and probably had numerous monthly subscriptions. Their approach to business management was different from mine. I believe in building a business on a solid customer base, where we either make a profit each month or cut back on expenses. It's a tough decision, but it's the right one.

Their business was built on the premise of a TV show, and they assumed that the traffic generated would convert into sales. They did get a lot of traffic and made sales, but I suspect they kept telling themselves that they would make the necessary sales the following month. In the meantime, they kept increasing their expenses. Eventually, they reached a point where they realized there was no return on their investment and had to stop, having run out of time.

Clues on what to sell

As a service provider specializing in web traffic, we informed our clients about the source of their site's traffic and what their visitors were searching for. These search terms served as hints for what products they should sell. However, we didn't handle their finances or business strategy. Our role was to provide advice, make recommendations, and offer assistance. Despite our long-term partnership, we never noticed any issues with their revenue. In fact, it seemed that they ran one of the most profitable websites on the internet, based on the data we had access to and their own reports.

The sales process, in essence, is quite straightforward. The market's behavior indicates what it is interested in. In this instance, it was home cooking. Everything related to home cooking was selling well then, as it is now. This includes cookware, cutlery, books, and many other products, all in high demand.

Any of these items could have been tested. A few calls could have been made to check prices and stock levels, and then offers could have been made just to gauge interest. They could have even offered premium, branded products. They had the chance to use the show's logo and its stars. The reason they didn't exploit these opportunities more remains a mystery to me.

Over the years, I've met several industry professionals who were part of a family that started a website. Many faced financial challenges, but they used their newfound knowledge to secure jobs in other companies. They aimed to learn more about the digital world, possibly with plans to make a comeback later.

I know many people who went to the city with a business plan but failed to secure the funding they needed. However, I did meet a few lucky ones who followed a path similar to mine. My business functioned as a supplier to gold miners, but we didn't mine the gold ourselves. Numerous service companies emerged, all eager to help customers improve sales, usability, and track user behavior. It seemed like everything could be managed, organized, and directed.

The city provided customers. There appeared to be plenty of money available for the gold diggers. Various trends came and went. Community, health, fitness, pets, fintech, and much more. Everything was becoming virtual, yet little seemed real. A true revolution had occurred.

Our website served as our storefront, and we ranked first in search results for decades. Our trading figures were also impressive. Customers are our everything.

Much of what we saw was fool's gold. Virtual services for virtual customers. It was easy to get swept up in the hype, and it's still the case today. The hype hasn't disappeared; it's as strong as ever, following today's trend and evolving into tomorrow's.

Many new businesses had excellent ideas, but few knew how to actively attract customers. Most believed in the "build it, and they will come" principle.

My goal was to attract customers who would make purchases. My test is simple: does a customer want to buy what's for sale? If not, what will they buy? They're buying something, so let's keep trying different offers until they buy from us.

Our main customer came to us by a happy coincidence, through a referral, and it wasn't even in the city. The sales director became aware of what we could offer through a conversation with his ex-wife, who worked for another of my businesses at the time.

During our first meeting, he told me what he wanted. We agreed that it was achievable, and he placed an order. We then had to quickly figure out how to fulfill the order. And we did.

It became clear to me what steps were necessary and how to execute them. However, it wasn't until I made my first order that I truly began to accomplish the necessary tasks. This wasn't about pretending until success was achieved. Instead, it was about securing a customer before making a significant investment. In essence, you don't have a business until you have a loyal customer. While ideas are plentiful, customers are scarce. Only when we understood the customer's needs could we start considering how to meet them.

While others focused on selling website designs, we prioritized delivering what the customer wanted to purchase. We discussed potential outcomes and results, inviting customers to share their desires. We knew what had been successful in the past, and now we're enjoying the process of working with clients and delivering the service.

We documented the case study and even created a few hypothetical use-cases to showcase potential achievements. We cautiously offered the service to other marketing directors, some of whom were eager to take us up on the offer.

The work was highly technical, but we only hinted at it without going into great detail. Our marketing and communication efforts emphasized the expected outcomes and results.

Demand is crucial, supply is manageable, but generating demand is the real challenge. We could direct many people to relevant sites to provide information and cater to their interests. The tricky part is converting these visitors into customers. We aim to provide an experience that aligns with our brand, but only after we understand what our visitors want to buy. Otherwise, we risk creating a brand experience for a brand without customers, which is pointless. Many business owners make the mistake of investing upfront, thinking it's crucial. The key is to understand if customers are interested, how they will express their interest, and how we can facilitate this process.

When you have an idea, the first step is to evaluate it as quickly and cost-effectively as possible.

Whether online or offline, we need to be agile and precise in all areas.

You've probably heard the phrase "new and exclusive". This is because the offer is new, and it's exclusive because only one is available. If the promoted item is successful, it's possible to create another, and another. Each item can be designed exclusively until it no longer is.

At each testing stage, you can modify the offer. You can adjust the price point, alter the design, or change the exclusivity. You should also consider feedback and reviews.

3 things you can test fast

Testing the market doesn't have to be expensive.

For start-ups on a tight budget, there are three things you can test quickly: personal services, information, and finished products. Personal services involve offering your time and skills to customers. The initial costs are typically minimal, as it's just your time and effort. If you manage to make a sale, you can consider hiring someone to help out. This is known as financing sales, which is generally a good strategy as you can borrow money knowing you'll get it back.

Information, such as guides, books, or coaching services, is another product you can test. You likely already have the knowledge needed, so it's just a matter of packaging it in a presentable way. This can yield high returns and quickly turn a small investment into a larger profit.

Finished products are another option. These are items you already have or can easily obtain or manufacture. Initially, you might do this as a side job to satisfy your primary customers. However, if the demand grows, it might become your main source of income.

Any of these three options could be a good starting point for a business. As your business grows, you'll likely need some cash to finance expansion and pay for services over time. However, even if growth is slow due to lack of funds, it's not necessarily a bad thing.

Having a backlog of customers is a good problem to have. It gives you the opportunity to adjust your prices based on what works best with your initial customers. You can offer different pricing options, such as a higher price for quick turnaround or a lower price for those willing to wait. You can also build a reputation for reliability and integrity by honoring your promises.

Your first customers might be lucky, as you might be willing to offer them special deals just to show that you value your customers. One way or another, you'll get to where you need to be.

Financing actual sales is less risky and easier than funding an unproven business. If you need cash to finance sales, it might be a sign of success. When customers want to buy from you faster than you can deliver, it's a good problem to have. Often, the solution is to increase prices to cover costs and compensate for the risk and additional financing costs involved in delivering the products.

Of course, mistakes are inevitable. I've hired the wrong people and paid for services and equipment that weren't effectively used. But I didn't take on any loans and signed only a few finance agreements. I did get stuck with a photocopier contract that my co-director signed while I was away, which was annoying but not too costly in the end.

I've invested and lost small amounts of money on projects that didn't pan out. But the important thing is to learn from these experiences. The only way to truly test a business is to see if customers will buy what you're selling. Being cost-conscious is good, but don't forget to factor in the cost of your time.

On the bright side, I learned valuable lessons and gained new skills, such as agile project management, which opened up new market opportunities. Despite some setbacks, I've had unexpected cash paydays after a year of effort.

Lean business principles

Lean business principles and agile development, typically associated with software companies, revolve around the concept of creating a minimum viable product (MVP). This principle isn't exclusive to software businesses and can be applied to any entrepreneurial venture.

In today's digital age, a website can serve as an MVP. It can be designed, developed, and launched swiftly and inexpensively, with the domain name often being the most costly component. However, with a bit of research, free domain names can be found. By utilizing server-less technologies, such as hosting on Amazon S3, the monthly maintenance costs of a website can be minimal. Moreover, if the business doesn't succeed, the absence of traffic means no ongoing costs.

A website can serve as an effective platform to showcase your MVP, engage with visitors, and experiment with strategies to convert them into customers. The beauty of this approach is that it can be executed with little to no financial investment. The success or failure of the venture depends more on the appeal of the offer than the money spent on the supporting technology.

Banks often provide funding for customer-based growth. However, startups can sometimes benefit from having little to no capital, as this minimizes the risk of financial loss. By meticulously assessing each cost and investing only in what's necessary, you're more likely to get exactly what you need.

The 5 steps to success with no money down:

1. A product or service

2. A marketing strategy that identifies potential customers and their motivations to buy.

3. A genuine interest or passion in the subject to keep you motivated over time.

4. The energy to execute your plans, which involves taking care of your physical and mental health, as well as your diet.

5. The ability to take action. This is often the most challenging step, as many fail to follow through.

Here are three crucial aspects of your lifestyle that you should pay attention to:

1. Be mindful of how you utilize your time.

2. Take on responsibility.

3. Only engage in activities that align with your values.

Time management is a critical aspect of success. It's not just about working harder, but working smarter. This could mean reducing the time spent on leisure activities like watching TV or going to the pub, depending on your local regulations. We are social beings and it's natural to want to spend time with friends and family.

However, to ensure the success of your future business and the well-being of your family, you must invest time in planning, strategizing, and refining your business model.

Avoid setting vague, money-centric goals. Instead, focus on the process and the details of each step. Ask yourself questions about your target customers, their buying habits, and how you can incentivize them to purchase more or refer others to your business. These considerations don't necessarily lead to costs, but if they do, evaluate if these costs are essential and if they can be deferred.

The second key aspect is embracing responsibility. Your success is solely up to you and blaming others or external circumstances won't help. Every business owner faces obstacles, and it's your responsibility to navigate through them. It's not a choice between running a business or maintaining personal relationships. The real challenge is finding a balance that allows you to do both. This might require making compromises, but taking responsibility will guide you through these tough decisions.

Starting a business can be an isolating experience, especially if those around you don't understand or support your endeavor. However, you must take charge of your circumstances and persist with your business, even if it's a no-money-down venture. Remember, you're not alone in this journey. Many have successfully established businesses before you, and you can learn from their experiences.

Balancing work and family life can be challenging. Your family should always be your priority, as the ultimate goal of your business is to provide a better life for them. Successful people take responsibility and manage their time effectively to cater to everyone's needs. This might require involving your family in decision-making to ensure everyone understands and is on board with your plans.

The third key aspect is belief. If you don't believe in what you're doing, you're likely to fail. However, if you face challenges but believe in your mission, you'll find the strength to persevere. If any part of your business goes against your values, stop immediately and find an alternative approach that aligns with your beliefs. Internal conflict can lead to loss of interest and belief in your business. If the means don't justify the ends, you must find a better way. Pause, rethink, retool, and restart.

Note that money is not a prerequisite for success and doesn't feature in any of these key aspects. In my experience, money usually comes from customers. If you take care of your customers, they'll take care of you.

When you encounter financial limitations, there are several strategies you can employ. For example, you can license a successful product or service in your local area to a distant location. Licensing not only provides a steady stream of income without the need for sales financing but also acts as an asset that can be further marketed.

Many businesses initially struggle to generate revenue, often due to their reliance on a single source of income. However, there's no rule that limits you to one income stream. You can establish multiple revenue channels to attract more customers. Some potential sources of income could include monetizing certain marketing channels, publishing a book on Amazon, running a YouTube channel, or starting a membership site. There are numerous such channels that can provide unexpected income.

It's crucial to diversify and establish multiple income streams as early as possible. Relying on a single income source can lead to difficulties if any issues arise. Often, when you're focused on delivering a product or service, you can't simultaneously sell it. Therefore, it's important for sales and marketing to run concurrently with production and delivery.

As a general guideline, I believe that marketing activities should take up no more than half a day at most. The idea is to engage in short-term tasks. For instance, creating a two-minute video might take half an hour of writing, filming, editing, and uploading. In a single morning, you could potentially create five or six videos, enough for six weeks if you release one video per week. You can even schedule the publication date for each video when you upload it.

If you're considering starting a YouTube channel, be prepared to consistently upload a video every week, and understand that it might take up to two years before you start earning from the traffic. If you're creating a product single-handedly, it could take a year or longer. With a partner, the process could be shortened to a few weeks or months. If you're offering a service, a well-planned meeting could secure a trial contract for a month. If you deliver excellent results and are well-prepared, the contract could potentially be extended. I prefer to have my clients pay monthly retainers whenever possible, as it allows me to plan ahead and increases the likelihood of success.

Continuing monthly contracts are highly valued, and many clients are keen to secure them because they guarantee a fixed price and offer stability for their businesses. This could be a solid foundation for your business as well.

However, in my haste to expand my business, I wouldn't hastily hire anyone. Instead, I would treat a new venture as a side project and encourage friends to join me, hoping it could turn into something more substantial. I would also recommend that clients pay at least 50% upfront and provide written orders.

Offering a money-back guarantee could be an option if you think it's feasible, although I've only ever done this for online (distance) sales, where it's mandatory.

If a client is unwilling to pay any money upfront, you run the risk of acquiring a client who never pays. This is a common issue for start-up business owners. Therefore, asking for money upfront is often crucial. It's important for a client to show commitment by having some stake in the project. You might prefer asking for a 50% deposit, or a guarantee, or for the funds to be held in escrow. Building trust is essential. Taking on a project for a client involves significant risk on your part. You need to be sure of a positive outcome and that the client is serious about the opportunity.

If you find it hard to ask for money upfront, consider how much harder it would be if the client didn't pay at all. Non-payment is a major issue for start-up business owners.

Another key point for start-ups is the risk of offering services for free. This can make you appear desperate, unworthy, and unlikely to deliver quality work. Moreover, if you only attract business by offering free services, you're not respecting the market's commercial value.

Offering a free service can hinder your progress, as you'll either have to fund it yourself or sacrifice your own time for no return. This is a significant one-sided investment.

It's important for a client to provide a written order for several reasons. Firstly, it can serve as a memento of your first order. Secondly, you can show it to suppliers, banks, and potential partners as proof that you have a client, which might encourage them to offer their support.

However, a written order should clearly outline expectations. Both parties should use clear, unambiguous language to describe exactly what is expected. This can be particularly helpful if there is a change in personnel, which can sometimes lead to non-payment.

Coming up next: Small steps can lead to big leaps. It's time to give yourself a raise and a promotion!

CHAPTER 6: FINANCING YOUR BUSINESS

Raising capital for a startup or for business expansion is essential. Depending on your business's nature, there are several methods to secure the required funds. Common financing methods include using personal savings, obtaining loans (debt financing), or selling shares of your business (equity financing). Other creative strategies such as using credit cards, crowdfunding, or purchase order financing can also be explored.

Getting a Business Loan

1.   Find suitable lenders: Business loans are a common method of financing. Reach out to banks you have a relationship with and ask about the procedure for securing a business loan.

2.   Small Business Administration (SBA): The SBA, while not a direct lender, offers loan guarantees for small businesses. This means that if you fail to repay the loan, the SBA will cover the repayment. Keep in mind that the definition of a "small" business varies based on your industry.

3.   Online lenders: Online lenders often have more relaxed loan requirements and may not require collateral. However, it's crucial to investigate their credibility by reaching out to the Better Business Bureau and local consumer protection groups.

4.   Prepare necessary paperwork: Lenders need to evaluate your company's financial health before granting a loan. Prepare

the following documents that are typically needed by most lenders:

o   Resumes of owners and management

o   Business and personal tax returns for the last three years

o   Personal and corporate bank statements

o   Credit reports

o   Company licenses

o   Articles of organization or incorporation

o   Commercial leases

5.   Keep financial reporting up-to-date: Most lenders also require financial information from your business. Make sure the following are prepared and regularly updated:

o   Personal financial statements certified by significant business owners (usually those owning more than 20% of the business)

o   Company balance sheet (overview of assets, liabilities, and owner equity)

o   Income statement (shows company profitability over a certain period)

o   Cash flow analysis

o   Check and correct any errors in your credit report before applying for a loan

6.   Provide collateral: Offering assets as collateral can make loan approval easier, especially if you don't have a credit history. Various assets such as property, vehicles, equipment, or other

valuables can be used as collateral. Talk to banks to understand specific requirements and appraisal procedures.

7.   Submit loan application: After submitting your application, the lender will review it and make a decision. This process usually takes two to four weeks. If you've applied to several lenders, compare loan details including interest rates, fees, early payment penalties, and repayment plans.

Finding Potential Investors

1. Identify suitable investors: Raising capital for your business can be achieved by selling shares. The choice of potential investors should be based on their relevance to your business, and there are different types and sizes of investors to consider.

o Colleagues: Think about partnering with colleagues who have the skills you lack, such as marketing or product development.

o General public: Publicly traded companies allow the general public to buy shares. This option requires legal consultation and a process with the Securities and Exchange Commission.

o Affluent individuals: Angel investors are wealthy people who invest in start-ups. They often expect a seat on the board or involvement in daily operations in return.

o Venture capital firms: These firms assess and invest in businesses, often playing an active role in decision-making and business expansion.

2. Understand the advantages and disadvantages of equity financing: Selling a portion of your business means acquiring more shareholders who are entitled to future earnings. They may also

have voting rights in business decisions and full access to your company's information.

o If you give up more than 50% of your company, you may lose control, but you won't need to return the money if your business fails.

Guidelines on Financing Your Business

Section 1: Various Business Financing Options

Capital is crucial for initiating a business and facilitating its growth. There are numerous methods to procure the funds required based on your business's unique needs. While self-financing is a traditional way, other prevalent options include debt financing (acquiring a loan) and equity financing (selling shares of your business). Additionally, innovative approaches such as using credit cards, crowdfunding, or purchase order financing can also be explored.

Section 2: Securing a Business Loan

Securing a loan is one of the most common ways to finance a business. Here are some steps to guide you through the process:

Identify potential lenders for businesses:

a. Commercial banks: If you already have a business account with a bank, you can approach them to inquire about a business loan.

b. Small Business Administration (SBA): While not a direct lender, the SBA guarantees loans for small businesses, meaning they will cover the cost if a business defaults on its loan. However, eligibility for SBA loans can differ based on your business type.

c. Online lenders: These lenders often have more relaxed loan requirements and may not ask for collateral. Nonetheless, it's crucial to verify the lender's credibility through platforms like the Better Business Bureau and local consumer protection agencies.

Prepare the required documentation:

Lenders need certain documents to evaluate your business's financial health before approving a loan. Ensure you have the following documents ready:

Resumes of owners and management

Business plans

Personal and business tax returns from the past three years

Personal and business banking statements

Credit reports

Business licenses

Articles of organization or incorporation

Commercial leases

Maintain up-to-date financial records:

Lenders will also require financial information from you. Ensure you create and regularly update the following records:

Personal financial statements certified by key business owners

Company's balance sheet summarizing assets, liabilities, and owner equity

Income statement illustrating the company's profitability over a certain period

Cash flow analysis

Review your credit report and rectify any errors before applying for a loan. Errors can comprise incorrect balances, credit limits, or accounts falsely reported as being in collections or default. You can rectify these errors by reaching out to the concerned credit bureau either online or via mail.

Secure pledgeable assets:

Offering assets as collateral can simplify the loan approval process, particularly if you lack a credit history. Various assets, such as your home, car, equipment, or other valuables, can be pledged as collateral. Consult with banks to understand their specific requirements, including any necessary appraisals.

Submit your loan application:

Once you've submitted your application, the lender will evaluate it and make a decision. Typically, it takes two to four weeks to receive a response. If you've applied to multiple lenders, compare the loan details, including interest rates, fees, early payment penalties, and repayment terms. Consider the overall cost and conditions before making a decision. Ensure the accuracy of the provided details and reach out to your loan officer if you have any queries. Submit the application along with all the required supporting documents.

Section 3: Attracting Investors

One method to secure funding for your enterprise is by enticing investors. Here are some steps to consider:

Identify potential investors:

Decide on the kind and size of investors you wish to target. Your options might include:

Colleagues: Think about collaborating with a colleague who has the expertise you require, such as in marketing, product development, or sales.

The public: If your enterprise is publicly traded, the general public can buy shares of your company on the stock market.

Angel investors: These are individuals who usually offer capital during the early stages of a business in return for equity or convertible debt.

Venture capitalists: VC firms put money into businesses with high growth potential in return for equity. They typically invest larger sums than angel investors.

Develop an engaging pitch:

Create a convincing and succinct pitch that emphasizes your business's unique selling propositions, growth prospects, and financial forecasts. Clearly state what differentiates your business from its rivals and how investors stand to gain by investing in your company.

Participate in networking and investor events:

Join networking functions, industry conferences, and startup contests to connect with potential investors. Establish relationships and seek introductions to investors via mutual contacts or professional networks.

Design an investor presentation:

Create a detailed investor presentation that presents your business model, market research, competitive analysis, financial forecasts, and funding needs. Utilize visual aids like charts and graphs to effectively communicate your message.

Present your pitch to investors:

Arrange meetings with potential investors to showcase your business and investment opportunity. Be ready to respond to queries about your business plan, market potential, revenue forecasts, and anticipated return on investment. Emphasize the main benefits and risks linked with investing in your business.

Negotiate terms and finalize the agreement:

If an investor shows interest, negotiate the investment terms, including the equity share, valuation, and any additional conditions or agreements. Get legal counsel to ensure the terms are equitable and align with your business objectives. Once both parties concur on the terms, complete the investment through legal paperwork and the transfer of funds.

Section 4: Other Ways to Finance Your Business

In addition to traditional loans and funding from investors, there are other ways to finance your business that you might want to consider:

Crowdfunding:

Through crowdfunding websites, you can solicit funds from a large group of people who each donate a small amount. You present your business idea or project on the site and offer perks or rewards to entice people to donate. Some of the most well-known crowdfunding sites are Kickstarter, Indiegogo, and GoFundMe.

Business Grants:

Look into grants that are offered by government agencies, nonprofit organizations, or private entities. These grants are usually given out based on certain criteria, like the type of industry, geographical location, or the social impact of the business. Be aware that the application process for grants can be rigorous and competitive.

Financing from Suppliers or Vendors:

Some suppliers or vendors might be willing to provide financing options to help you buy their goods or services. This kind of agreement lets you delay payment or set up a payment schedule.

Bootstrapping:

Bootstrapping is when you finance your business yourself, using your personal savings, credit cards, or revenue from early sales. Although it requires careful financial management, bootstrapping lets you keep complete control of your business without taking on debt or giving up equity.

Keep in mind, the way you choose to finance your business should be in line with your business objectives, financial requirements, and risk tolerance. You might want to consider getting professional advice from financial advisors, lawyers, or business consultants to help you navigate the process.

CHAPTER 7: GAINING NEW CLIENTS TO EXPAND YOUR CUSTOMER BASE

As an entrepreneur, I've faced numerous obstacles throughout my journey. I've learned the importance of gaining new customers, particularly during periods of scarcity. In this section, I'll share my personal experiences and insights on how to establish and expand a business, even in the most difficult situations. I never anticipated that my path would lead me to author a book, but I'm excited to share my knowledge with budding entrepreneurs like you.

The process of gaining new customers is a critical part of any business. It involves persuading potential customers to select your products or services over others. This process requires a well-planned strategy that draws in leads, nurtures them, and eventually converts them into devoted customers. The expense linked with these activities, referred to as the client acquisition cost (CAC), is a crucial factor to consider.

Attracting new clients is vital for businesses of all sizes and stages. It not only generates income to maintain your operations and facilitate growth, but it also serves as a testament to your success for potential partners, investors, and influencers. Regularly attracting and converting new customers satisfies investors and enhances your business's overall reputation.

Through customer acquisition, you create a systematic plan to draw in clients and ensure your business's longevity. Relying on customers to find you organically is an option, but it doesn't guarantee steady profits over time. This is where customer acquisition specialists step in, using specific strategies to encourage potential customers to act.

It's crucial to understand that customer acquisition extends beyond traditional marketing. While marketing increases awareness, customer acquisition aims to inspire action. For example, if you run a Facebook ad targeting your desired audience, marketing analytics can gauge the success of your campaign. However, acquisition refers to what happens when potential customers engage with your ads, visit your website, or interact with your emails. When a customer decides to buy, that's when acquisition occurs, generating revenue for your business.

You might be curious about the difference between lead generation and customer acquisition. Let's delve deeper into this concept. The customer acquisition funnel is a model commonly used to understand the customer journey in the business world. It outlines the steps involved in the buying process and the strategic thinking of potential customers.

As customers move through the funnel, they become more familiar with your brand, consider your product or service as a potential purchase, and ultimately decide to do business with you. Lead generation, lead acquisition, and lead conversion occur at different stages of the funnel. However, it's vital to see the entire process of attracting and acquiring customers as the full customer acquisition funnel.

Acquisition marketing concentrates on creating ad and marketing campaigns that target consumers who are already aware of your brand and considering a purchase. It sets itself apart from other types of advertising by focusing on converting prospects who are aware of your business.

In the current digital era, digital acquisition marketing plays a significant role. Using online channels such as display ads, social media, and organic search, it aims to attract and target new customers. Collaboration between your marketing and customer service teams is essential for a successful digital acquisition strategy.

Your marketing team works diligently to create and disseminate captivating promotional materials to pique the interest of potential customers. Simultaneously, your customer service representatives, who are in direct contact with your existing clients, can also play a crucial role in attracting and retaining new customers. The collaboration between these teams ensures that your customer acquisition marketing efforts go beyond the boundaries of traditional marketing.

Apart from organic search and digital strategies, businesses employ various customer acquisition methods like email marketing, organic social media, and paid advertising. Each method has its unique advantages and is effective in different situations. By understanding your target audience, available resources, and overall business strategy, you can identify the most suitable acquisition approach for your company.

Organic search, or SEO (Search Engine Optimization), involves enhancing your content to achieve higher rankings on search engine results pages (SERPs). By focusing on relevant keywords and producing engaging content, you can draw in potential customers who are actively looking for products or services similar to yours. Tools such as Open Site Explorer, SEMRush, and Ahrefs can assist you in pinpointing the perfect keywords for your business and improving your organic search visibility.

Pay-Per-Click (PPC) advertising is another beneficial paid search marketing method. With PPC, you create targeted ads that appear alongside organic search results. By bidding on keywords related to your business, you enhance your visibility and the likelihood of being found by potential customers. Platforms like Google Advertising and Microsoft Advertising offer tools to enhance your PPC campaigns and boost performance.

Acquisition marketing also encompasses the digital sphere, using channels like social media and display ads to attract and engage new customers. By harnessing the power of social media platforms and creating compelling content, you can increase brand awareness and captivate your target audience. The synergy between your marketing and customer service teams ensures a smooth experience for potential customers, whether they're browsing your website, interacting with your live chat, or reaching out via social media.

As you delve into various customer acquisition methods, it's crucial to strike the right balance between paid and organic strategies, inbound and outbound tactics, and available resources. Your acquisition strategy should align with your target market's preferences and behaviors, and be flexible enough to adapt to changing market conditions and trends.

In this chapter, I've imparted valuable insights into customer acquisition, drawing from my own experiences as a successful entrepreneur. By grasping the principles of customer acquisition, reducing costs, and maximizing the value of your existing clientele, you can formulate a flexible and effective acquisition strategy that propels your business forward.

Remember, acquiring new customers is not just about increasing revenue, but also about forming enduring relationships and laying a solid foundation for future growth. By investing in customer acquisition and consistently delivering value, you can position your business for long-term success.

Now, equipped with this knowledge, it's time to act and commence your customer acquisition journey. The potential is limitless, and I'm eager to see the growth and success you'll achieve. Let's dive in and acquire those new customers who will drive your business's expansion and pave the way for a brighter future.

As a prominent businessperson and expert in customer acquisition, I've had the opportunity to explore a variety of strategies within the ever-changing world of social media marketing. In this section, I will explore the world of organic social media platforms, sharing my personal experiences and insights on how to use these platforms effectively for customer acquisition.

Social media marketing can be divided into two types: free and paid. Both have their advantages, but organic social media offers unique opportunities to increase brand recognition, develop a business persona, and share content from other sources like blogs or videos. Consider it as a way to fuel a fire that you've already started using other acquisition strategies.

One of the main benefits of organic social media is its potential to go viral. By encouraging your clients and followers to share your brand's news, you can utilize the power of word-of-mouth marketing. It's amazing how a single share can dramatically increase your reach and attract new customers.

However, depending on your budget and target audience, using paid social media platforms may be a more appropriate choice for your business. Investing in social media visibility and advertisements ensures that you reach your targeted audience without needing to build a large following of loyal fans. While building such a following is still crucial, paid social media can give an extra push to your customer acquisition efforts.

To effectively manage and schedule your social media content, I suggest using a free calendar template and management tool. This will help you stay organized and maintain a regular presence on social media platforms.

Sponsored posts on social media do more than just deliver content. They allow you to collect important user data such as names and email addresses from your audience. This information is more than just content delivery; it helps you differentiate between a lead and a follower. Platforms like Facebook Lead Ads can be very useful in obtaining valuable leads for your business.

Email marketing, although considered outdated by some, is still an extremely effective customer acquisition strategy. It provides a direct link to your customers' inboxes, allowing you to communicate with them and convert them effectively. Through email, you can provide great content, product details, discounts, and updates on events. It also serves as a platform for meaningful interactions with your target audience, whether it's sending a birthday message or a thought-provoking marketing email.

Unlike other marketing channels like search or social media, email marketing establishes a direct communication line with your customers. It is one of the most powerful customer acquisition methods, second only to direct sales. To effectively leverage email marketing, you need to build an email list and use it as a powerful marketing tool.

Referrals, often an underestimated source of customer acquisition, can be a game-changer. Your existing customers are the key to attracting new ones. While you can't force your current clients to refer others, you can foster an environment that encourages and rewards them for doing so. Setting up a referral program is a proven method to acquire more customers through recommendations. By offering rewards and compensation, you can motivate your customers to promote your brand. Ensure that the value you offer in return reflects the significance you attach to a customer referral.

Events such as conferences, webinars, and trade shows are excellent platforms for meeting potential customers and growing your business. In our digital era, virtual events have become increasingly popular, making it easier to gain customers who register with their email addresses. Hosting virtual summits or webinars, or securing a booth at a larger event, can be a key strategy in your customer acquisition plan.

Despite the dominance of digital marketing, traditional marketing channels like TV, radio, and print media maintain their significance. These channels can be highly beneficial for both small and large businesses, as long as your ads are targeted effectively. For instance, TV ads allow you to reach a broad audience and harness the power of visual storytelling. This can be especially powerful for brands aiming to showcase their products or stir emotions through compelling narratives. Radio provides a platform to connect with listeners via audio ads, which can be effective for targeting specific demographics or geographic regions.

Print media, including newspapers, magazines, and direct mail, can also be a crucial part of your marketing strategy. They provide a tangible and credible platform to communicate your brand's message and reach audiences who prefer reading offline. Print ads can be strategically positioned in publications that cater to your target market, ensuring your message is received by the right audience.

When considering traditional marketing channels, it's important to thoroughly understand your target market, their media consumption habits, and the effectiveness of each channel. Moreover, integrating traditional and digital marketing strategies can result in a comprehensive and unified approach, maximizing your reach and impact.

Keep in mind, the effectiveness of traditional marketing channels can vary based on your industry, target audience, and budget. It's vital to monitor and measure the outcomes of your campaigns to calculate their ROI and make data-driven decisions about your marketing mix.

In summary, while digital marketing is crucial in our connected world, traditional marketing channels like TV, radio, and print media still hold value. By understanding your target audience, customizing your message, and selecting the right channels, you can harness the power of traditional marketing to supplement your digital efforts and achieve your marketing goals.

Organic social media is the lifeblood of contemporary marketing. As an entrepreneur, I've seen the remarkable influence it can have on businesses. Social media marketing comes in two forms: free and paid. Today, I want to focus on organic social media and discuss how it can drive your business's growth.

Organic social media is about building brand awareness, infusing personality into your business, and sharing valuable content that already exists elsewhere in the digital world—like your blog or videos. Consider it as fueling a fire that you've already started using other acquisition strategies. It enables you to harness the viral effect, motivating your clients and followers to organically spread the word about your brand.

However, we shouldn't overlook the potential of paid social media. Depending on your budget and target market, using paid platforms might be a more strategic choice for your business. Investing in social media visibility and ads ensures that your message reaches your audience without the need to painstakingly build a dedicated fan base (although, let's be real, that's important too).

In order to optimize your social media activities, you need to be well-organized and have a schedule. Luckily, there are free calendar templates and management tools available to make your social media content more efficient. Use sponsored posts to your advantage, as they not only deliver your content to the right people but also collect useful user information like names and email addresses. Facebook Lead Ads, for instance, are a powerful tool for social media advertising and simultaneously help you build your contact list, which is crucial for distinguishing between potential customers and mere followers.

Email marketing, an old yet effective tool, is still a highly efficient strategy for acquiring customers. It allows you to stay in touch with your audience by providing them with high-quality content, product details, discounts, and updates about events. Email bypasses the constraints of search algorithms, social media algorithms, and content saturation, providing a direct line to your customers' inboxes. It's the second most effective method of customer acquisition, trailing only behind direct sales.

So, what do marketers do with all the customer data they collect from various acquisition methods? They compile an email list and utilize its power as a marketing tool. Email marketing offers unmatched opportunities to engage with your target audience. From sending personalized birthday messages to crafting informative marketing emails, it's a channel that lets you customize your messaging to cater to each customer's specific needs.

Referrals are a hidden gem in your customer acquisition toolkit. Sometimes, the most effective strategies are right under your nose, concealed within your existing customer base. One of the most effective ways to draw in new customers is by leveraging customer referrals. While you can't force your current customers to refer you to others, you can definitely foster an environment that encourages and rewards their advocacy.

Creating a referral program is a proven strategy for gaining more customers through word-of-mouth. By offering incentives like credits, physical gifts, or cash rewards, you inspire your customers to share your brand with others. Remember, if you highly value a customer's referral, make sure to give back something of similar value. B2C companies often thrive with structured, incentive-based referral programs, while B2B businesses may benefit more from directly asking for customer referrals. Regardless of the path you choose, always focus on providing value before asking for anything. Give your customers a reason to endorse you, and when they are satisfied with your products or services, they will naturally become your brand's ambassadors.

Events are an ideal platform for meeting potential clients and securing new business. Conferences, webinars, and trade shows provide excellent opportunities to interact with your target audience. Even in this digital era, face-to-face communication still holds immense value. Events allow you to display your products or services, engage in meaningful discussions, and form personal bonds with potential customers.

To maximize the benefits of events, start by identifying the conferences, trade shows, or industry events that cater to your target audience. Investigate their attendees, topics, and opportunities for involvement. Decide whether it's more beneficial to participate as an exhibitor, speaker, or sponsor, based on your objectives and budget.

When you're at events, make sure your booth design is eye-catching, your presentations are engaging, and your materials are informative. Create a welcoming environment that piques the interest of attendees and encourages them to learn more about your brand. Offer interactive activities, demonstrations, or samples to create a memorable experience.

Networking is crucial at these events. Establish connections with industry professionals, potential clients, and thought leaders. Engage in meaningful conversations, actively listen, and exchange contact details. After the event, follow up with personalized emails or calls to nurture these relationships.

Remember, events aren't just physical gatherings. Webinars and virtual conferences are becoming more popular, providing a convenient and cost-effective way to engage with a broader audience. Use technology to your advantage by hosting webinars or participating in virtual events, broadening your reach and connecting with potential clients worldwide.

In conclusion, organic social media, email marketing, customer referrals, and events are all effective customer acquisition strategies. By strategically using these methods, you can increase your brand's visibility, build genuine relationships, and ultimately boost your business growth. Embrace the opportunities provided by digital platforms, while also appreciating the importance of in-person interactions. Tailor your approach based on your target market, industry, and resources, and continually assess and refine your strategies to maximize your customer acquisition efforts.

A sustainable client acquisition strategy is one that ensures long-term effectiveness. It involves investing resources like money, time, and personnel in a manner that can be maintained for the foreseeable future. For example, if you choose to use a blog to attract more customers, you need to have the necessary resources and tools to regularly publish valuable content that generates organic traffic over a sustained period. Inbound marketing is a perfect example of a sustainable approach since it consistently attracts visitors and maintains a steady influx of new customers. On the other hand, commercials may be effective in the short term but may not be sustainable in the long run.

Adaptability is key in the ever-evolving marketing landscape. With constant changes in consumer behavior and market trends, a flexible client acquisition strategy is essential. In the past, salespeople were the main source of product information, but today, consumers are more skeptical of brand claims. Relying solely on salespeople for customer acquisition can be risky. By ensuring your strategy is adaptable, you can continually adjust it to align with changing market conditions and evolving consumer preferences.

Understanding your target market is crucial for effective customer acquisition. Not every customer is your ideal customer, so if your efforts are not focused on the right audience, they can end up being a waste of resources. Before investing in any client acquisition techniques, it's vital to define your target market. Creating buyer personas can help you eliminate inefficient or unnecessary acquisition efforts and better understand the specific needs and preferences that certain channels can fulfill. Taking the time to establish a targeted customer acquisition strategy allows you to make informed decisions that align with your business, resources, and audience, leading to measurable results.

Diversifying your client acquisition approach can bring significant benefits. Just as cross-pollination leads to stronger plant species, diversifying your acquisition strategy and using a variety of approaches increases your chances of reaching new audiences and generating new leads. It also balances risk and reward, making it easier to shift investments to a different, higher-performing strategy if one channel underperforms.

Keeping track of each customer's lifetime value is essential for sustained success. While drawing in new customers is vital, maintaining their loyalty is even more important. Identifying customer segments that show high loyalty can enhance your overall plan and the effectiveness of your customer acquisition initiatives. Customer lifetime value (CLV) is the expected net profit a person or business will bring during their tenure as a paying customer. Although calculating CLV can be complex, it offers useful insights into customer habits, directs marketing activities, and impacts business choices. Customers with high CLV might be costlier to acquire initially, but they surpass other customers in revenue generation, referrals, and feedback. This allows for a more efficient use of their acquisition budget, leading to a higher return on investment and improved business outcomes.

By evaluating CLV along with the cost of customer acquisition (CAC), businesses can figure out the time needed to recoup their investment in new customers. This facilitates better decision-making and resource distribution.

In conclusion, a sustainable client acquisition strategy requires investment in long-term tactics. Having the necessary resources, adapting to market changes, understanding your target audience, diversifying your strategy, and keeping an eye on customer lifetime value all play a role in creating a successful client acquisition strategy that delivers enduring results.

CHAPTER 8: THINK BIG, START SMALL, SCALE FAST

Freedom at last

The initial step is to jot down your entrepreneurial ideas and thoughts, no matter how outlandish they may seem. Begin by listing your interests, without worrying about organization or coherence. The key is to get your thoughts on paper, you can refine them later.

As you embark on your entrepreneurial journey, you'll have the freedom to choose your own path. It's important to pick something you're passionate about, as this enthusiasm will fuel your journey.

Throughout your life, you've been taught what to learn and how to think. Now, it's time to break free and focus on your own desires. This is why writing down your thoughts is crucial. Your future is all about you and your aspirations.

The dark side

There will be naysayers who will try to discourage you, telling you that you're out of your depth or that you don't deserve success. They might question your authority to advise a client or a CEO.

Your family might have conditioned you against entrepreneurship, especially if they've always been employees or if your family has traditionally been against individual success and capitalism.

You might have seen the inefficiencies of bureaucracy, the wastage of resources, and the poor returns of state-owned utilities. You might have experienced the harshness of debt collectors who consider you guilty until proven innocent.

There will be challenging times filled with doubt, frustration, and unhappiness. But these periods are usually short-lived, especially if you love what you do. Consider starting in an area you enjoy and see if you can merge your passion with your business. Enthusiasm is a powerful tool during tough times.

If you've been in a profession for a long time and enjoy it, consider transitioning into consulting. For instance, if you're a dentist or lawyer, you could help others in your field run their practices or attract clients.

Optimism is key. When one door closes, two more usually open. The important thing is not what obstacles you face, but how you overcome them. When unexpected things happen, think about how you can turn them to your advantage.

In the beginning, it's easy to take setbacks personally. But dwelling on them only hinders progress. Accept that things can go wrong, and if they do, take responsibility and fix them as quickly as possible. Remember, you can overcome almost any problem with the right resources.

When things go awry, don't play the blame game. Accept it, find a solution, and keep moving forward. As long as you have a positive cash flow, you can resolve the issue and continue on your journey. Remember, setbacks are a part of the entrepreneurial journey.

Most people in business are good people. Keep this in mind during tough times. Stay resilient, don't give up too soon, and be prepared for unexpected challenges.

How To Think Big, Start Small And Scale Fast

The concept of thinking big but starting small is something we all can relate to. Usually, we begin with minor steps or set incremental goals. The quickest way to scale is by getting customers to pay upfront, which is a common practice in the online world. The majority of the exponential growth we've seen recently has been in the digital space.

Starting small typically means we aim to impress someone with our abilities or skills. Once we've done that, it's easier to believe there are more such opportunities out there. We begin by focusing on a select few.

Even if we come up with a grand idea, like creating a viral internet sensation, it's still wise to start small. Starting small allows us to gather feedback and adjust our approach accordingly.

It's crucial to take the time to develop a high-quality, reliable product or service that satisfies customers and allows the business to scale to meet their needs. Without a good product or service, you could quickly find yourself in trouble. Initially, you'll likely only cater to a few small clients. To expand, you'll need to completely revamp your offerings. Your first clients are likely to be early adopters who are willing to take a risk. These individuals are often eager to be at the forefront of new developments and may account for up to 20% of the market.

As time goes on, your client base will become more mainstream, comprising up to 60% of the market. These customers are less interested in personal connections and more focused on getting the job done. The last 20% of the market is made up of laggards who demand proven products with solid guarantees and are willing to pay the lowest price. These customers may not be your favorites!

You'll find that some customers, from each group, will stick with you for a long time. Each group has different reasons for choosing you. The first group may notice many changes in you and may even reminisce about the past.

It's important to identify and manage each customer group based on their perception of you. If you stray too far from their view, they may look for other options. It's crucial to maintain relationships with past clients to prevent competitors from swooping in.

Mass marketing is a delicate process. Take Intuit, one of the largest online software suppliers, as an example. Despite their size, they focus heavily on the small details. They have a program called 'follow the customer home', where they work closely with customers to understand their needs and use their feedback to improve their software continuously.

There are some exceptions to the rule. Take Kentucky Fried Chicken (KFC) for example. Despite many fast-food outlets selling similar products, KFC has managed to stand out. However, even with their 'special' recipe, they haven't been able to prevent others from selling similar products.

Businesses like these are hard to protect as they can be easily copied. Even the secret recipes of Coca-Cola and KFC haven't stopped others from producing similar products.

Personally, I prefer smaller markets with a few frequent spenders rather than many who spend little. However, it's worth noting that these massive chains all started from a single outlet.

Who are you for?

Various niche groups exist that possess significant purchasing power. It's a smart strategy to identify and cater to these specific groups as it can help you maintain their loyalty over time. Ideally, you want your customers to perceive that you are there to serve them.

Being customer-centric involves a certain level of personalization, which can help you become the preferred choice in your market. By creating customized resources, you can generate unique intellectual property (IP) tailored specifically for them. This strategy effectively creates a protective barrier around each customer group, making it difficult for competitors to infiltrate.

When you define who your target audience is, you are better able to understand their specific needs. This focused approach allows you to showcase specialized knowledge that potential customers will acknowledge and appreciate. Customers generally prefer businesses that understand their needs and believe that such businesses can serve them more efficiently. If you can prove your expertise and capabilities, your target audience will trust you to guide them towards success.

Your specialized knowledge, capabilities, and experience can discourage customers from switching to competitors, as they wouldn't want to miss out on what you offer. You can leverage this inherent appeal to make it challenging for customers to replicate your business unless they have a license.

Licensing is one of the quickest ways to expand a business. It's a win-win situation for everyone involved. It's a cost-effective marketing strategy that also offers privacy - two significant benefits for any start-up. It allows you to maximize revenue and profits without revealing your trade secrets.

These principles can be implemented in almost any business. They are commonly used in most start-up ventures or market opportunities, with a few exceptions.

Avoiding Risk

Markets with extremely high values, often in the millions, are usually characterized by high risk and incredibly low profit margins. The stakes are high, with vast sums of money involved and slim margins for error. A small mistake can result in significant financial loss. This high-stress environment often leads many to abandon certain business ventures due to the elevated risk associated with large sums of money.

Big numbers tend to attract those who are drawn to the allure of wealth. However, it's possible to accumulate substantial profits through smaller customer projects that carry less risk. By spreading smaller amounts of risk across multiple customers, a potential disaster won't spell the end of your business. While all losses should be avoided, a minor loss only results in a temporary decrease in profits, unlike a major disaster.

The key takeaway is that a more relaxed, less risky life can be achieved by diversifying your client base to include more low-risk clients. Otherwise, you may find yourself years into a business where one huge, "sure thing" gamble could wipe out all your profits.

It's also important to diversify your business activities. Perhaps focus on three or four areas simultaneously. Start with an area that interests you and then expand to other diverse markets.

For example, if you want to monetize a podcast, you could:

• Choose your favorite topic and target three related audience groups.

• Offer three types of products: a starter package, a monthly package, and a premium package, each at different price points.

• The packages could be essentially the same for each market, with only the name changing to suit the target audience.

Take some time to plan how you would monetize a podcast using this model. This method costs nothing, but it can help you create an appealing offer in multiple ways. It also significantly increases your chances of success while reducing your risk.

This approach is not only cost-effective and quick, but it also reduces your dependence on a single type of client, marketing strategy, or delivery method. You'll quickly find out where your potential clients are and secure your business with multiple income streams.

Monetizing a podcast is just the beginning. You could run the podcast by yourself or interview experts. You could also transcribe the audio, edit the content, and use it in a guide, book, or as part of an online delivery. This topic and its potential for income generation is explored in greater depth in the members' area online.

Business risks need to be continually evaluated. Over time, most people tend to become more risk-averse. The worst scenario in business is being reliant on one - one market, one service, one client, one boss, one invoice. Why risk everything on high-risk clients or projects, especially when the outcome is supposedly guaranteed?

If you value your peace of mind, avoid putting all your eggs in one basket. Yes, you need your first customer, but you should quickly strive to secure your second, third, and fourth. By broadening your scope, you can secure more clients. After all, if you managed to get the first one, you can certainly get more.

Scale

To me, scale signifies the ability to generate a significant amount of revenue. How much is significant? It's an amount that exceeds our needs. The concept of scale primarily revolves around the ability to increase sales with ease, and the most effective way to do this is by systematically utilizing resources and seeking synergies.

In essence, business is about creating value. We don't necessarily have to personally solve problems; it's enough to know someone who can. Can we provide similar assistance to others? What additional services can we offer our target market? Ideally, we should aim to expand by focusing on our top three priorities, systematizing them, and then moving on to the next set of priorities.

Identifying customer needs or areas of difficulty becomes easier with experience. As you gain more practice, you'll become more adept at spotting these opportunities.

When it comes to scaling, it's often more beneficial to provide tools for others to succeed. Instead of being pioneers, we can focus on areas of high interest and assist people in their pursuits. For example, in the world of bitcoin, it might be more profitable to aid bitcoin investors than to invest in bitcoin yourself.

In every market, there's a top 20 percent of high-paying clients. These are the clients you should get to know well. A business needs a system to filter sales and select the most suitable clients to work with.

Consider this: as an author, you write a book once, but it can be sold thousands of times. Similarly, once a webpage is coded, it rarely needs to be redone. Some of these visitors will find what they're looking for, and some of them might want more. This is where the 80:20 rule comes into play.

It's always better when clients come to you. Outsourcing can help prevent resources, time, and money from being stretched thin. Book sales on Amazon is a prime example of effective outsourcing. Amazon markets the books, collects the payment, delivers the product, and pays the remaining amount to the author. This process can generate a substantial passive income.

Passive income is the ideal scenario. Book sales not only generate income but also direct customers to you. Many people are seeking passive income, and it's right in front of them. Writing and selling books on Amazon is a straightforward way to generate passive income. It's simple, makes sense, and can attract a large audience.

Both passive income and becoming an author are scalable. However, they shouldn't be the only focus. For example, interviewing experts can provide valuable insights about your target market and create content for a podcast or similar platform.

The goal is to create versatile content that can be used in various ways, such as advertisements, special reports, videos, articles, and online membership areas.

Writing is a crucial skill for making money. Before I wrote my first book, I knew technical authors and copywriters who wrote marketing stories, direct mail, and brochures. They never taught me how to write, but reading their work and observing their techniques helped me pick up the skills. Start collecting interesting pieces for future reference. Good writers often start as avid readers.

Practicing writing through social media posts, emails, and post replies can also be beneficial. Writing a book is about organizing your thoughts on one or two topics you're passionate about. It's a peaceful activity that costs virtually nothing and involves minimal stress.

Planning a book becomes easier when you write bullet points on familiar subjects. The book practically writes itself and really starts to take shape during the editing process. If you're considering writing a book, think of it as an extended PowerPoint presentation. Bullet points are like seeds that can grow as much as your enthusiasm allows.

The purpose of this proposal is to share insights on how to start a business without any initial investment, a strategy I've used to launch all my businesses. Understandably, this topic piques a lot of interest. By sharing my experiences, this book has gained visibility. Some readers might want to collaborate with you, purchase more of your books, or refer you or your books to others. This process is mutually beneficial and everyone benefits.

Even if the book doesn't result in sales or new clients, it's not a big deal. If the book doesn't do well, there's no need to feel embarrassed as no one will notice. But if it's well received, that's a bonus.

Some readers will benefit more than others. Those who want to delve deeper can visit the book's accompanying website. This method is effective as it avoids aggressive sales techniques, allowing you to engage with readers and potentially attract those seeking further assistance.

It's impossible to satisfy everyone all the time (just ask any politician, though some are admittedly in denial). Some people may not appreciate your transparency, while others might find your ideas too basic. But if you're sincere in your efforts to help readers, chances are it will be very successful.

There's so much you can do. You can write a book, create a PowerPoint presentation, host a webinar, start a podcast, launch a membership website, distribute free software, or document business processes. Creating assets is highly scalable, and most can be delivered digitally, which can help your business gain popularity.

Remember, you're not just creating assets from your imagination or research. Documenting systematic business processes is another way to create an asset. A system asset is something you can use and potentially license to others, either as a blueprint they can follow or as an outsourced service your team provides.

We're at an interesting crossroads. Some people might relate to this, while others might find it foreign. We might be using unfamiliar language or referencing unknown places. The content might seem too complex. The author is a man, the reader is a woman, etc. It's easier for most of us to find reasons not to act rather than to act. We tend to focus on differences rather than similarities.

A better approach is to view objections as challenges and think about how you can apply these ideas in your own world. This mindset can take you much further.

If this seems overwhelming, revisit the ideas. Select the ones that resonate with you the most and prioritize them. Focus on the top three and once you've accomplished those, reassess your list. It's unrealistic to try to do everything at once, but it's entirely possible to tackle a few ideas at a time.

Some might argue these suggestions won't work in their market. However, adopting an idea from one industry and applying it to another where it hasn't been used before is a common way to become a millionaire. This is the essence of innovation, a key aspect of business. Your future isn't about what you have or what you like, it's about how you can make what you find beneficial for your customers.

Sales

Success in business is largely dependent on our ability to sell and attract new customers. As entrepreneurs, selling is an integral part of our role, although it often gets a bad rap due to the negative stereotypes associated with salespeople. However, selling is about facilitating a customer's purchase, not about being greedy or pushy.

Think back to your childhood when you persuaded your parents to buy you an ice cream on a hot day. That was selling. Similarly, when you make a good first impression or present an idea persuasively, you're selling. It's a skill we all have and use, often without realizing it.

In essence, selling is about engaging with people in a friendly manner. It doesn't require aggressive persuasion. In fact, you can often sell more by simply guiding people on what to do. For example, suggesting someone read a particular book before starting a business. If you're interested in refining your persuasive skills, I recommend reading Persuasion by Robert Cialdini.

Personally, I find Neuro-Linguistic Programming (NLP) more useful, despite its negative reputation. The techniques are natural and not overly manipulative. However, like anything, they can be overused and make you come across as too pushy.

If your product or service is genuinely good, you won't need to resort to high-pressure sales tactics. In my experience, these tactics are often counterproductive, especially if the customer is already interested in what you're offering.

We often feel the need to push potential customers to make a purchase immediately. For me, this is usually due to time constraints. However, the most effective strategy is to attract customers to you. When customers seek you out, they're more likely to be ready to buy. They want what you're offering, they respect you, or they've been referred to you. In these cases, there's no need for hard sell tactics. In fact, using them could even cost you sales.

The ultimate sales technique

Despite our expertise, we often make the same avoidable mistakes. Many common issues could be prevented with the right approach. The good news is that there's a simple process that can help you communicate your message effectively and avoid these pitfalls.

The first step is to make it clear that you have a solution to a problem and that you offer a free initial consultation. This is a win-win situation. Sometimes, a quick fix is all that's needed, which can boost your reputation and generate referrals. Other times, a more comprehensive solution is required, which can lead to significant problem-solving opportunities.

Offering a free consultation is a strategy used by many professionals. It's an effective way to attract potential customers and showcase your expertise.

Why should you offer an initial free consultation?

Whether it's a doctor, lawyer, or insurance broker, the first meeting typically involves a free evaluation of your needs. This consultation allows you to discuss your problem with a professional who can provide further insights. The information shared during this session may help you understand whether your issue needs urgent attention or if it will resolve on its own.

Consultations are generally a comforting experience, as they often lead to the discovery of new strategies to mitigate the problem or lessen its effects. The expected adverse impact is reduced, and a clear path forward is established.

Every situation is unique. Individual consultations promote clear communication focused on the primary concerns, tailored to the participants' desired outcomes and the consultant's expertise. A successful consultation should lead to a mutual understanding of whether the consultant has the necessary expertise to address the concern. If not, a referral to a consultant with the relevant experience is usually the next step. However, such referrals are rare and typically occur in highly technical cases. Most of the time, the necessary expertise is found, and potential solutions are discussed.

Personalization is key

If you're looking at this from an advisory standpoint, such as in health or cybersecurity, the goal is to have your advice heard and implemented. The process involves identifying the objective and discussing the best ways to achieve it while maintaining a robust health or cybersecurity stance.

From a sales perspective, understanding the needs and objectives allows you to offer a solution that closely aligns with the core requirements, leading to a successful sale. In both scenarios, all parties can be satisfied, and this is how advice is not only heard but also acted upon.

In some cases, a more in-depth examination of the facts may be necessary to ensure all aspects are thoroughly investigated, increasing the likelihood that the proposed solution will work. This is often followed by a proposal or detailed prescription, with the terms often being interchangeable.

Further questions may arise, and adjustments or modifications will be made to accommodate them. Some solutions may be automated, while others may require manual intervention. This is similar in both health and business scenarios.

Avoid the forced imperative

Imposed obligations are typically unwelcome and seldom implemented. A consultative approach is particularly effective in these situations. Ignoring consultation can lead to more issues and increased costs, as everyone is given the same take-it-or-leave-it solution, resulting in decreased acceptance. Ensuring compliance becomes challenging, especially when the only options are coercion or failure. In the business sector, customers have the choice to change providers and often do so without hesitation.

A good bedside manner instills good feelings

A competent doctor is often praised for their good bedside manner, which doesn't necessarily reflect their technical skills. However, it greatly influences the results and trust patients have in them. Better treatment might seem like an illusion, but it likely reduces service costs and increases overall patient (client) satisfaction. The key difference is the personalized consultation. This is why some restaurants are perceived as superior, even when the food quality is the same. The distinguishing factor is the individual attention provided by the waiter.

The waiter's prism

Looking at the waiter's role through the lens of giving advice and having that advice followed, we can understand why this role is beneficial for business, even though the waiter is not involved in food preparation. The waiter usually greets new customers at the entrance, embodies the business's image, and immediately asks a question after a warm welcome. The question could be how they can assist or what the customer is looking for, or they might offer to guide the customer to a table. Regardless, it's a straightforward question that addresses the customer's needs and is promptly acted upon. The customer is then personally escorted to a table.

The waiter continues to inquire about the customer's requirements, timing, and possibly arranges the table and initial beverages, such as offering a water carafe. This is the consultation phase where the waiter caters to the customer's needs, discovers how they can assist, and actually helps them.

Customers will soon feel comfortable ordering food from the menu and probably appreciate the waiter's suggestions, who is knowledgeable and can make recommendations to ensure the customer's comfort and optimize the restaurant's kitchen operations. This leads to satisfied customers, good revenue, and the possibility of repeat visits.

The advantage of a low-pressure sales approach

There's no need to pressure anyone into making a purchase at any given time. Customers come seeking service, and if it's provided effectively, they'll stay. However, if the service is lacking or they're enticed elsewhere, they'll move on. If they choose to stay and utilize the service, it's because it resonated with them and met their needs.

A high-quality consultation prevents manipulation

There's no aggressive selling or obligation to purchase, as simply providing a valuable service can create a win-win situation. Offering genuine and compassionate assistance forms a solid foundation for building goodwill, leading more people to follow your advice. More people will recommend you and spread the word about your expertise in your field. Ideally, the consultation experience will contribute to creating a positive narrative about their experience working with you. This is the kind of narrative you want to circulate. This is why this is the ultimate guide to attract potential customers, engage them with your message, and motivate them to act.

Next up: What to sell and when to sell it: you may face challenging times before experiencing the joy of success. Don't succumb to unforeseen pressures. There will be some adjustments to make when it comes to serving customers. You'll have the opportunity to define your startup's identity, which will provide insights into how to position your business and identify potential customers.

The following chapter will guide you away from potential pitfalls and disasters. This is precisely why it's crucial to know where these pitfalls lie and have strategies to avoid them.

CONCLUSION

We've established that the primary focus should be on acquiring a customer. We've discussed the significant advantages that a customer brings to your business. We've shown how having a customer is the crucial factor that differentiates a business from a hobby. While this knowledge is often sufficient for those in the initial stages of setting up a business, there's more to it.

Entrepreneurs in the early stages of their start-up often overlook the necessity of having a customer. We tend to get lost in the intricacies of setting up the business, the exciting technology involved, or the skills needed to accomplish our goals. These elements are undoubtedly exciting, but customers are the ones who demand results.

Many start-ups make the mistake of chasing an ideal vision. However, it's the customers who truly represent the unique group of people who can help turn your vision into reality. Therefore, the sooner you acquire a customer, the sooner you can validate whether your vision is something they would be interested in purchasing. At any point, you may need to adjust your approach to make your vision a reality, and feedback is always valuable.

We can all agree that time and money are resources we never seem to have enough of. We all want more. Interestingly, focusing on the customer can also lead to more money. When our attention is on the customer, we tend to ignore other distractions.

A customer is the key to providing you with everything you need and more.

As your start-up grows and attracts more customers, your customer-related goals are likely to evolve. Initially, your business is unique and unknown, but over time, it will become reliable and established. As a start-up entrepreneur, you need to be prepared for these changes.

It's important to dedicate time to creating assets. Customers themselves are assets. They can be managed to develop your intellectual property and market positioning. The continuous development of assets will ultimately help you demonstrate why you are the best option for your customers. Whenever possible, assets should be shareable and have the potential to go viral, helping to spread the word and generate excitement in the market.

You will need to change and adapt

Initially, you might cater to a specific customer segment that is easy to please, generating immediate cash flow and buying you time. Ideally, you will satisfy enough customers to finance the next phase of your business. This success should enable you to shift your focus to customers who align more closely with your ultimate business vision. Remember, the journey to success isn't always a straight line.

As you begin to gain your first customers, take the time to work closely with them to ensure you can meet their needs effectively. Strive to exceed their expectations to ensure their complete satisfaction. This could lead to testimonials, the ability to create use cases, or even customer-approved testimonials and case studies, with their consent.

As your business progresses, your offerings will evolve and expand, opening up new market opportunities. You will also need to create efficient, cost-effective sales systems and processes to attract new customers. Simultaneously, you will learn to identify your high-value customers and develop a scalable method to convert customers into clients.

Gradual growth will put pressure on other aspects of your business, necessitating increased overheads and improved cash flow management. You will discover more effective ways to finance sales based on your understanding of client behavior. These challenges need careful management as your business transitions from start-up to a more established entity.

Over time, you will find innovative ways to position your stories and assets in the market.

You will need to improve your ability to exceed expectations and gain a better understanding of your target audience. You will identify the markets where you fit best and understand why customers choose you. This knowledge will make it easier for you to generate more sales and grow your business.

You will begin to establish a reputation in the market, possibly in a new niche or an emerging market. You will gain a better understanding of your market positioning and find ways to enhance it. Your focus will gradually shift to a group of potential customers who are abundant and willing to do business with you. They, in turn, will find it easy to perceive you positively.

Competence, confidence, and capability

As time passes, your business should continue to grow.

The more you tailor your offerings to your customers, the more likely you are to convert them into clients. You will start securing long-term contracts, with some clients placing ongoing or rolling orders. As your business matures, some banks may start to view you favorably, potentially offering financial services to support your customer and client needs, which can significantly aid your growth.

In the early stages, don't anticipate too much financial assistance.

Help usually becomes available once you can demonstrate a steady client base and repeat business.

You should be proud of your achievements so far. Many people never receive the recognition they deserve for their hard work. Most people think you're simply doing what you're supposed to do, and after all, you're making money from it, right?

So, let me take this opportunity to congratulate you on your success. I understand how challenging it can be, even if it might seem easy on the surface.

www.ingramcontent.com/pod-product-compliance
Lightning Source LLC
Chambersburg PA
CBHW072217290526
45794CB00004B/1777